THRESHOLD TO TOMORROW

BY RUTH MONTGOMERY

RUTH MONTGOMERY

THRESHOLD TO TOMORROW

G. P. PUTNAM'S SONS / NEW YORK

Library of Congress Cataloging in Publication Data

Montgomery, Ruth Shick, date.
Threshold to tomorrow.

Continues: Strangers among us.
1. Occult sciences.   2. Reincarnation—Case
studies.   I. Title.
BF1999.M739   1983   133.9′01′3   82-10172
ISBN 0-399-12759-3

Printed in the United States of America

To "Laura"

Who opened the door
for the Walk-ins to stride forth

CONTENTS

settlements
+167

FOREWORD

If you have not already met a Walk-in, you soon will.

They are everywhere, and, according to the Guides, are harbingers of a new order that will bring peace on earth in the twenty-first century.

While writing *Strangers Among Us*, which introduced the subject of Walk-ins, I felt remarkably privileged to know three of those seemingly unique individuals who had entered adult bodies in order to serve humanity.

Nowadays I seem to be stumbling into Walk-ins wherever I go. I have spoken with dozens of them, which is scarcely surprising because the Guides say that tens of thousands of them are already in physical being throughout the world. "They are New Age

9

disciples," they declare, "who are returning at an accelerated pace to usher us into the Age of Aquarius when all will be as one, and the biblical prophecy of the millennium will be fulfilled."

Walk-ins are idealistic but not perfected souls, who, through spiritual growth in previous incarnations, have earned the right to take over unwanted bodies, if their overriding goal is to help mankind. The original occupants vacate the bodies because they no longer can maintain the physical spark of life or because they are so dispirited that they earnestly wish to leave.

The Guides, to whom readers of my previous books need no introduction, are souls, like ourselves, who have lived innumerable earth lives but are currently in the spirit plane, as you and I will be when we eventually pass through the door called death. Actually, those in spirit are simply functioning at a higher vibratory level, and the particular group that communicates with me through automatic writing each morning has taken on that long-term project in the hope of awakening us earthlings to the reality of a richer life beyond our five senses and our three-dimensional world.

In the three years since publication of my last book, the public seems to have become ready to acknowledge the existence of the so-called strangers among us. Wherever I lecture throughout the country, hands invariably are raised when I ask if any of those in the audience believe that they know a Walk-in.

Even the often pragmatic medical profession is beginning to recognize the feasibility of a soul-transfer-

ral to explain the remarkable alterations in character
and personality that follow many near-death experiences, and some outstanding psychiatrists are quoted
on the subject in this book. As one of them views it:
In this era, when transplants of kidneys and hearts
are becoming commonplace, why should it be difficult to believe in body transplants as well?

In *Strangers Among Us* it was essential to disguise
the identities of Walk-ins until people could become
accustomed to the concept and accept the fact that
they are not mysterious aliens but high-minded individuals who willingly accepted the challenge to put
damaged bodies back into working order or to heal
the psyche of emotionally disturbed people who
wanted to abandon the mess in which they found
themselves. The Walk-ins replace the Walk-outs, not
for the questionable pleasure of assuming secondhand bodies, but to assist mankind in preparing
for the difficult times said to be facing all of us.

We are in a race against time, and these enlightened souls are therefore permitted to forego the
time-consuming process of babyhood, childhood,
and schooldays in order to launch their projects for
the benefit of humanity, and to save us from ourselves. Only eighteen years remain before the long-
predicted shift of the earth on its axis, and in preparation the Walk-ins are beginning to make their
identities known, so that they can find each other
and work more effectively as a group to harness our
collective energies. By no means are all of them towering leaders. If you learn through this book to recognize Walk-ins, you will encounter them driving
taxis, clerking in stores, serving on city councils,

teaching classes, working in factories, and engaged in similar endeavors where they can quietly influence others to help one another and prepare for the dark days ahead.

The Guides declare that many people who survive clinical death are actually Walk-ins, and because they are coming directly from the highly energized spirit plane they are able to revive and utilize bodies that would otherwise be wasted.

They also attest that some who call themselves born-again Christians are in fact different, rather than reformed, souls. But certainly not all of them. To illustrate, they say that former president Jimmy Carter is not a Walk-in, but that certain other born-again persons are. At my lectures I am invariably asked whether Charles ("Chuck") Colson is a Walk-in, because of his startling alteration of character following the Watergate debacle. The Guides insist that he is, although the former "hatchet man" of the Nixon White House, who has subsequently devoted his time to converting hardened criminals, believes that he is simply "born again in Jesus Christ."

Because my husband and I were living in Cuernavaca, Mexico, throughout the Nixon administration, I am hazy on the day-to-day details of the Watergate scandals, and, except for President Nixon, I have no firsthand acquaintanceship with the cast of characters, as I would have had if I was still covering Washington for my syndicated political column during that era. By the time we returned to Washington, Watergate had become old hat, and I did not bother to follow the spate of books that were being published about it.

Intrigued by the Guides' assertion that Charles W. Colson was actually a different soul from the one who had served Nixon so unquestioningly, I asked if they could pinpoint when such an alleged transferral occurred. "In the driveway," they replied. "A good example of a Walk-in replacing a departing soul who was sick at heart and unable to face the disgrace and the future."

This seemed a strange response to a question asking for specifics. What on earth could have happened in a driveway to evoke such a cryptic reply? Determined to track down the clue, I visited the public library and checked out several books about Watergate. After skimming through them without finding an allusion to a driveway, I learned that Colson had written an autobiography some years ago, titled *Born Again*. Securing a copy, I waded through the early part of the book, which sketches his youthful years, his duties as adviser to the president, and the ugly details of the attempted Watergate cover-up. Then he described his own shame and despair as the vise closed around him, and finally a visit to the New England home of Tom Phillips, president of Raytheon Company, who told Colson that he had undergone "the most marvelous experience" of his life when he committed himself to Jesus Christ. Phillips suggested that they pray together, but when it was his turn to pray, Chuck could not do so. He said good-bye, and went outside to his car, where the "iron grip" that he had held on his emotions relaxed, and he began to sob. He set his car in motion, but as he drove out of the driveway the tears were "flowing so uncontrollably" that he pulled to the side of the road. Then he started to pray, repeating over and over again the words, "Take me. Take me." And he told God that he wanted to "give myself to You."

The Guides have stressed that except in the case of a dying individual, a Walk-in will not enter a body unless the occupant asks to leave. It would seem that the emotionally exhausted Charles Colson, by his repeated pleas for God to take him, was doing just that. Certainly by his own account he became a changed person from that moment. A member of the Ervin investigating committee described him at his next session of testimony as "subdued and contrite," rather than defiant, and Colson wrote of himself, "Everything was different, much different from before, before Watergate, before any time I could remember. Even the people in the lobby of my office building seemed friendly, probably because I really looked at them for the first time."

Colson manfully served his prison sentence, becoming friends with many of the hardened inmates, and has since devoted all of his time to Prison Fellowship, an organization he founded to help the incarcerated find their way back to God. The Guides say of Chuck's transition: "He was desperate, afraid, and unwilling to face his family and friends. He withdrew with relief as he subconsciously realized that another with stronger morality and better grace would enter the body. He is here now in spirit, fascinated by his observations of the one who became Chuck Colson as far as the world is concerned, and pleased that he is doing so much to help others along the way. The one who entered and is now called Chuck Colson was a highly developed soul who in a previous lifetime had worked with indigents in England and made a real name for himself. He also had once served a prison term, through little fault of his own, but only because former English laws dealt so harshly with those who stole even a loaf of bread to feed their children and themselves. He will go far. The world has not heard the last of this reincarnated Walk-in."

At some lectures I am also asked about Harold Hughes, the former Democratic governor of Iowa and U.S. senator who abruptly announced in 1973 that he would retire from the Senate at the end of his term, although he was almost assured of reelection. It was no secret to his constituents that Hughes, a former infantryman in World War II, was a reformed alcoholic, and he had enjoyed enormous political popularity before quitting office to devote himself to helping other alcoholics find new direction for their lives.

The Guides said that Hughes is indeed a Walk-in, and that the transferral occurred "during an extremely bad bout" with the bottle. They added that he had "already determined during sober moments that he was unable to handle his life problem, and while under the influence of alcohol he subconsciously decided to withdraw and make his body available for a fine and well-integrated soul to take over and begin the process of assistance to others in like circumstances."

I had not known that Hughes and Colson, former antagonists from opposing political parties, had subsequently become friends, until I read the Colson autobiography. By time both would have been

Walk-ins, and Hughes had founded a halfway house in Maryland for alcoholics who were striving to overcome their addiction. Chuck wrote that the men met frequently at Fellowship House, a religious headquarters, for prayer sessions. Then he recorded this thumbnail sketch of Harold Hughes, which seemed to confirm what the Guides had written several months before I saw the book:

After his wartime service, Hughes "became a truck driver and an alcoholic, brawling his way from one bar to the next, sometimes gone from his young family for days on end, and often waking up from a drunken stupor to find himself in a strange hotel hundreds of miles from home. He often thought of suicide. Alone late one night in 1954 Hughes cried out to God for help. When the fog lifted the next day from his whiskey-soaked brain, everything around him seemed new. He never took another drink." Colson went on to outline Hughes's successful political career, which he then gave up because he "felt that his political life was in conflict with his commitment to Christ."

Hughes's attitude toward politics seems to have undergone another change in 1982, when he filed to run for governor of Iowa, but could not fulfill the residence requirement because he had too recently returned there from Maryland. The Guides predict that Hughes will again attain high office, and it is perhaps significant to note that in *Strangers Among Us* they declared that a Walk-in will be elected president of the United States later in this century, and that voters will be fully aware of his status.

The Guides have previously mentioned such biblical Walk-ins as Moses, Lot, Joseph with his coat of many colors, the Christ Spirit that descended into Jesus of Nazareth at the time of His baptism, and such historical ones as Christopher Columbus, Abraham Lincoln and Mohandas K. Gandhi. They now say that a particularly brilliant galaxy of Walk-ins returned to physical being before the American Revolution to help establish a new nation dedicated to the principles of equality, fraternity, and freedom of worship. Among those named are Benjamin Franklin, George Washington, Thomas Jefferson, Alexander Hamilton, James Madison, and Abigail Adams, but not her husband and son, who respectively became the second and sixth presidents of the United States.

From time to time friends and readers of my books have asked me if a certain individual is a Walk-in, and more often than not the Guides have replied in the negative. When queried about President Ronald Reagan, they said that he is the original occupant of his body, but they volunteered the information that in a previous incarnation he was Patrick Henry, the Virginia patriot-orator whose "If this be treason" speech gave powerful impetus to the movement resulting in the American Revolution. "That is why Reagan feels so strongly about returning to the original principles of the Republic and abhors big government," they added. Apparently, then, Patrick Henry's beliefs as well as his personal charisma have carried over into the new incarnation.

Others whom the Guides identified as natural-born individuals rather than Walk-ins are Israel's Golda Meir, China's Deng Xiaoping (Teng Hsiao-ping), General "Vinegar Joe" Stilwell, Charles Lindbergh, Admiral Hyman Rickover, Carol Burnett, Mother Theresa, Winston Churchill and Franklin D. Roosevelt.

But when I asked about the founders of three widespread religions, the Guides replied in the affirmative, saying that Mary Baker Eddy (Christian Science), Joseph Smith (Mormon), and Muhammad (Moslem) were all Walk-ins who came directly from the spirit plane to establish their precepts.

In dozens of interviews with Walk-ins, I have noted certain traits that they have in common. All of them believe in the Creative Force we call God, and speak of Him naturally, without embarrassment. They are modest, unassuming, and helpful. They seem to love their fellow human beings, even the most intransigent ones, and speak softly of "unconditional love." Certainly Christ gave that challenge to all of us when, in Matthew 5:44, he said, "But I say unto you, love your enemies, bless them that curse you, do good to them that hate you, and pray for them which despitefully use you, and persecute you."

In the pages that follow, we will see that Walk-ins have excellent factual recall, because they inherit the memory patterns of the predecessor that are impressed on the physical brain, but they encounter difficulty in remembering incidents having to do with the emotions of the Walk-out. Perhaps this can be compared with a computer, which has a stored memory that can be tapped by a person other than the one who fed the material into it but cannot reproduce the original programmer's emotional attitudes.

Divorce has figured largely in the lives of many who undergo soul transferrals. Sometimes it is the breakup of a marriage that prompts the Walk-out to withdraw. Other times it results from the inability of a spouse to live with an entity different from the original occupant of the body. Occasionally a marriage is strengthened by the transition, as the marital partner realizes that he or she is reaping an unexpected bonus in an improved mate.

According to the Guides, Walk-ins have been among us since mankind's advent on this planet but, because of the approaching shift, the pace of their return has been accelerated at a rate not encountered since the closing days of Atlantis, the legendary continent that disappeared beneath the Atlantic ocean some 12,000 years ago. Their task then was to preserve lives, documents, and the nucleus of civilization, as it is today; our modern Walk-ins are intent on teaching us the skills for survival, the philosophy of helpful community living, an awareness of safe areas, and the overriding importance of peace.

The Guides say of their mission: "They are harbingers of the New Age, messengers arriving to bring the word of how to free oneself from death and the passage into spirit. They wish to rid people of any fear of the shift, since it will usher in the beautiful age of the millennium."

But they stress that "Walk-ins are not necessarily superior, and certainly not perfected souls. They have their foibles and idiosyncrasies, and should not be condemned because they are less than perfect, for they too are still striving toward the perfection that leads to reunion with the Creator. They are, however, filled with a sense of purpose and an urgency to get on with the task of helping mankind and saving planet Earth in these coming decades. They feel that time is short, and their frustration with their inability, at times, to discover their mission is self-evident. They want to be of assistance to their fellowman, but because of their high-mindedness feel loathe to assert themselves and tender unsought advice. They need help from others, just as they wish to give help, and should not be castigated if they occasionally backslide, or get off to a slow start."

I asked my spirit pen pals what they foresee in the immediate future for Walk-ins, and they replied: "They are concentrating on bringing together in harmony those who are preparing for the changes to come, and are guiding many of them in their roles as teachers and workers in the vineyard. Some are starting New Age communities and assisting those already begun, but most are gently guiding others in the path of fellowship and self-help. They form a nucleus around which people are gathering, and these acolytes in turn will help others, just as the ripples widen in a pond when a pebble is cast into it. Their influence is spreading, and some will enter political life here and in other nations to influence corrective legislation and preparations for the difficult times ahead. Many of them are already in public office and in board rooms and teaching positions, and these numbers will increase as the time approaches when all must pitch in to save themselves and others. Mankind is indeed at a crossroads. Whether there will be war or peace is up to humanity, because all of us have free will, but we must learn to exert it for the common good."

For this book I have tried to select those cases that best typify the wide range of roles that Walk-ins are assuming and the various stages of their advancement. Due to the limited space, I have not been able to include all of those who were willing to be interviewed or to follow through on some of the cases reported to me by psychic friends. Gary Wayne, a Houston radio host on station KTRH who is himself a sensitive and who accurately predicted the assassination attempt on President Reagan and other electrifying occurrences only days beforehand on his radio show, has discovered a number of Walk-ins since the publication of *Strangers Among Us*. A woman psychic in New York who had never heard of Walk-ins said that while giving a reading for a young man she startled herself by declaring, "You are not the same soul who was born in this body." She reported his reply: "I know that, but you're the first person who has picked up on it."

A few Walk-ins are not yet ready to declare themselves publicly because of their present employment. One has a television show on the West Coast, and before the transferral of egos hosted a popular game show on a national TV network. Another man, who was sent home by his doctors twenty years ago to die, experienced enroute a blinding light that illumined all the space around him, and upon returning to his family told his wife in some bewilderment, "I know

I'm not the same soul that was in this body." He re-covered, and is now fully aware of his Walk-in status, but because he was and is a Baptist minister in the Deep South he does not want to imperil his family's livelihood by speaking out at this time.

Some of the Walk-ins, according to the Guides, have not yet found their particular mission, while others are already casting long shadows ahead, as they quietly seek to alert us to the roles that we too can fill in the coming decades. For those who are already engaged in public work, their addresses are included after the last chapter, so that they can be contacted directly.

And now—the Walk-ins!

CHAPTER I

JASON WINTERS*

It is possible that Jason Winters has been an instrument in effecting more remissions from the mysterious malady called cancer than any other single individual living today. Yet he is neither a doctor nor a scientist, and his formal schooling ended at the age of fourteen.

I had not heard of him until the spring of 1981, when, after reading *Strangers Among Us*, he wrote to me saying: "Four years ago I had terminal cancer of the tongue and jawbone, and a large malignant tumor under my ear. It was a hopeless case, although the doctors nevertheless insisted that they remove the jawbone, tongue, and possibly the voice box. But

*G. P. Putnam's Sons makes no representation, warranty, or endorsement as to the content of this chapter.

first I had to have a biopsy to find the extent of the cancer. The surgeons said it would take a half hour, but I was six and a half hours on the operating table, just for the biopsy. The cancer was too extensive to operate right away, so they decided to give me seventy-five radiation treatments on my face. I was never supposed to be able to use my tongue again, because they had cut the nerve during the biopsy."

Jason said that before the cancer he was an uneducated salesman and stuntman, always broke and always traveling. "My knowledge was limited. I had a great wife and five children, and was always worried about making ends meet. After the biopsy operation I was markedly changed. I found that I had a great knowledge of herbs and the natural way to live. I combined the herbs that I found around the world, and my cancer disappeared. I became fantastically healthy. Write-ups about me in magazines brought others to me, and all were helped.

"I began traveling the world, lecturing and bringing hope to millions. One and a half million people now use my herb formula, and the amazing results are all documented. Did something happen to me on that operating table? I quit school at the age of fourteen and never had further studies, yet I began to write. Suddenly I could converse intelligently with doctors, surgeons, and nutritionists. How can I explain my sudden interest in spiritual things, and the abrupt changes in my attitude and personality? Everyone notices the many differences in me. My wife was the first to notice and tell others about it, even before we read your book. Could you ask your friends [the Guides] if I am a Walk-in?"

Since publication of *Strangers Among Us* in the fall of 1979, I have received many letters from readers who implore me to ask the Guides if they are Walk-ins, but in most cases I am told they are not. When I asked about this particular letter writer, the Guides emphatically replied: "Jason Winters is indeed a Walk-in. He will go far in assisting others. That is why he came back."

Thus began my correspondence with this remarkable man, whose herbal tea and enzymes are sold in twenty-one countries to a million and a half people, nearly all by word of mouth. Even the medical profession is apparently taking notice. Jason says that his herbal formula is now being recommended by five or six hundred doctors in the United States, an equal number in England, and numerous others in Canada, and that Dr. Ian Pierce of England gives it to all his cancer patients.

According to Jason, the tea, which consists of herbs grown on three different continents, simply purifies the blood so that the pancreas can produce enough enzymes to devour the poisons in the system, and he says there are 30,000 documented cases in America alone of those who have experienced remission of cancer by drinking several cups a day.

There is no question that Jason Winters himself, in 1976, was a dying man. A team of doctors and surgeons pronounced him a terminal case, with infiltrating squamous cell carcinoma of his tongue, jawbone, and throat. The six-and-a-half-hour exploratory operation to take a biopsy disclosed that the malignant tumor was wrapped around his carotid artery and attached to the wall of his jugular vein. The team gave him three months to live if he agreed to massive surgery, or only days if he refused.

What they did not realize was that the badly frightened patient who had entered the operating room was now replaced by another ego who had just begun to fight.

Jason Winters was born in England on September 13, 1930, to a working-class family, and was seventeen years old before he rode in an automobile or ate in a restaurant. That was the year he and his parents moved to Canada to be near his two older sisters, who had married Canadian soldiers during World War II. Then began an adventuresome life during which Jason crossed the Canadian Rockies by balloon, traversed the MacKenzie River by canoe to the Arctic Ocean, hunted polar bears in Alaska and kangaroos in Australia. He spear-fished with the Maoris, crashed Jaguar cars through brick walls to test safety belts for the New Zealand government, crossed the Sahara Desert by camel, and went to Hollywood where he played the role of Geronimo in *Apache Agent* and performed as a stunt man in Audie Murphy films.

In Hollywood he met Jeannette, a stunning model who had emigrated from England in 1946, and after marrying they continued their restless wandering, with their five children being born in three different countries. "I was always poor," Winters says in retrospect, "but I was having a ball. Everything was fun, until I developed emphysema from smoking so much, a year before the biopsy, and became depressed and run down."

While taking a steam bath at the YMCA one

morning, he noticed a swelling on the side of his neck, and an ache deep inside his throat. He bought some lozenges and tried to forget it, but he couldn't help noticing that the lump was growing, and within a few weeks even his friends were calling it to his attention. Finally he went to his family doctor and was sent by him to a surgeon, who arranged for dozens of X-rays, scans, examinations at the Nuclear Medicine Center, and pills.

Then came the biopsy operation, during which a different soul reportedly replaced that of the discouraged man on the operating table. The Guides say of that transition: "In a previous lifetime the new Jason Winters had been a renowned healer in Australia, and before that an herbalist in England, where he taught and lectured on the use of natural foods and nature healings. He was also an astronomer in a lifetime in Italy, and has had a distinguished career in other fields of endeavor. He wanted to make use of his healing knowledge at this particular time, because the medical profession has become so devoted to chemicals manufactured by man, and in some areas so commercialized, that he feared the undoing of healing advances of the past. He entered the body of Jason Winters during the long drawn-out biopsy operation, when it became apparent to those on this side [the spirit plane] that the one then occupying the body would be unable to keep it alive for more than a few weeks. The new personality entered in order to rehabilitate the body and use its mechanism to help others overcome the same sort of physical ills from which the original Jason was suffering, and he has done so. He awak-

ened interested in anciently known herbs for healing, and brought them together into one channel
that has enormous restorative powers, and with his
fresh awareness he was able to infuse others with his
own enthusiasm and ability to live at peace with nature and the natural elements."

Before telling Jason about this message, I asked
him to describe the alteration of personality that
seemed to have occurred during that exploratory
operation. Without hesitation, he replied: "I entered
the hospital a nervous and frightened man. After six
and a half hours I awoke to the news of terminal
cancer with calmness, able to cope. Every morning
since then I have awakened with the same dream
memory. A man's voice is echoing in my mind.
There is a green hill with one large tree at the top,
and a man in a white robe is standing under the tree,
lecturing to dozens of us who are sitting on the
grass. The scene is beautiful, with colors far more
lovely than here on earth."

The Guides say that because Walk-ins bring in
fresh awareness, they subconsciously maintain contact with the spirit plane. It would appear that Jason
continues to receive instructions during the sleep
state, from former associates on the spirit plane, and
although his conscious mind does not recall the sub-
stance of the spirit lectures, the inner knowledge remains, to be used in the waking state.

The remarkable recovery of Jason Winters is described in a little booklet he wrote called *Killing Cancer*. In it he recounts how his doctor, after informing
him that he had terminal cancer, left him to his misery, and his wife, Jan, sadly went home to break the

news to their five children. But when the doctor made his hospital rounds the next morning, he found Jason and another patient engaged in "a hilarious pillow fight from our wheelchairs."

"The doctor was furious," Jason recalls. "'Don't you know you have terminal cancer? Don't you realize you should be in bed?' Because I was sure that all doctors were gods, I obeyed him quickly. But it was not long before I was out of bed again—this time to trudge around the hospital. I walked around the whole place five times for exercise, and when I returned it was the head nurse's turn to be furious. She said the doctor had been complaining to her about me, and once again assured me that I had terminal cancer. It seemed to me that everyone was worried in case I forgot to die. The doctor even went so far as to lecture my wife on my behavior."

Jason says that after numerous tests the medical team decided that he should have five weeks of cobalt radiation on his neck and head. Then, if the swelling went down sufficiently, he could have radical neck surgery. "That meant the removal of my tongue, jawbone, neck muscles, and the inside of my throat," he says. "To begin with I would receive three cobalt treatments each day for five weeks. The cobalt treatment took away my taste, made it impossible for me to make saliva, burned the right side of my face, and made my hair on that side fall out. I went from 263 pounds down to 170. My knees were shaky, and I could not stay awake longer than four hours at a time."

Through some inner prompting, Jason began eating spoonsful of honey after each cobalt treatment and smearing his burned face with vitamin E. Many of his fellow patients under cobalt treatment were dying, but he was improving to such an extent that the doctors remarked on how well he was withstanding the radical treatments.

"I told them what I was doing," he said with a grin, "and they said that was fine, but not to mention it to the other patients. That remark puzzled me no end. I *did* tell the others about it, and they all started the same treatment, with good results. I began to realize that doctors are not gods after all. They kept telling me to get my affairs in order and prepare to die, but I decided that perhaps I didn't have to die after all.

"The next day the surgeon called me into his office. He had decided to operate on me as soon as possible. Radical neck surgery. Removal of tongue, jawbone, and neck muscles. When I asked him if I would live any longer from having surgery, he said probably not. I looked him straight in the eye and said, 'No surgery.' Then I stood up and walked out of his office. My heart was singing. I was going to keep my tongue and if necessary, die in one piece.

"Many times the doctor called my wife to tell her to get me into the hospital. Everyone was trying to get me there, even though everyone knew that I would die anyway. I couldn't understand it. I wondered who these people thought they were, asking me to have this terrible operation."

Determined to survive intact, Jason Winters then went the Laetrile route, and for a time with good results. The tumor rapidly diminished, but after a time came back to its original size. Jason says of this disappointment: "It was as though I had been given life only to have it snatched away again. This time I really did prepare to die. I purchased all kinds of religious books, and while my family went to work to keep groceries on the table, I read them all. In my misery I was struck by how many times herbs are mentioned in the Bible. Herbs as medicines show up in so many different religions that it seemed to be too much of a coincidence. Hippocrates, the father of medicine, stated that herbs shall be for medicine. So did Buddha and Krishna. Then I found that the American Indians believed in herbs and used them as medicine; also the gypsies of Europe, and the Hunzas, and the aborigines."

From his readings he decided that the most powerful ancient herb for tumors was a root that grows only in Asia, but his long-distance calls failed to locate any of the herb in the American marketplace. Then he learned that it was available in Singapore, and with one of his children supporting him under each arm he made the grueling flight. Shortly after arrival in Singapore his wife located an old woman in a rural area who cultivated the herb recommended by the Buddha for tumors, and for two weeks he drank the mixture steeped in hot water. At the end of that period, although the tumor had not noticeably enlarged, it also had not reduced in size. They purchased some more of the herb to take with them and flew next to Tucson, Arizona, where Jason located the herb known as chaparral, from the creosote bush, which Mexican Indians drink for health, and he tried brewing that, but with no better results.

Then, with his money all but gone, he used his

credit cards to fly to England where he was introduced to red clover *(Trifolium pratense,)* the gypsy
health drink, and spent the next few days brewing
clover blossoms tea, then the Asian herb tea, and
then the chaparral. By the fourth day he was so desperately ill that his wife insisted on their returning to
America while he still had enough strength to travel.
After returning home Jason went back to brewing
his three kinds of herbal tea, and laboriously wash-
ing out the teapot after making each variety, but experiencing no improvement.

"I was busy making tea and drinking it all day
long, and getting weaker all the time," he recalls.
"One morning I was at my lowest ebb. I thought, To
heck with it, I'll mix all the herbs together and save
time. I'll never forget that it was five minutes to ten
on a Wednesday morning. I made the tea combination and a miracle happened. I could feel it with that
first swallow. It seemed to ring a distant bell, and
awaken a long-ago memory. It screamed at me that
this was what I needed. Strength seemed to pour
into my body. That day I made a gallon of the tea
and drank it all."

When his family returned to the house they could
see the difference in him, and knew that something
remarkable had happened. Jason was jubilant. He
knew now that he was going to live. He continued
mixing the teas together, and within three weeks the
unsightly tumor had vanished from his neck. In nine
weeks he returned to work, feeling healthier than he
had since his youth. His friends were amazed, and as
word spread throughout the community, people
with cancer began thronging his doorway. He had

given some of the tea mixture to his parish priest, and when the padre's hemorrhoids, from which he had suffered for twenty years, disappeared within two weeks of tea drinking, he told Jason that he must make the tea available on a wider scale, even though he could expect persecution and ridicule from the pharmaceutical and medical professions, or be guilty of the sin of omission.

"After much thought I decided to tell my story," Jason says. "A small newspaper first took up the story, which resulted in over three hundred telephone calls and a thousand letters, plus a bigger lineup outside the door from 8:00 A.M. until past midnight. My boss fired me because I was supposed to sell refrigerators, but cancer patients filled the store and we could not move. Everyone wanted the tea. Separately the herbs would not work for me. Together they were a miracle. I started importing the ingredients and mixing them in four-ounce bags, which I would give to anyone who wanted some. In exchange they would make a donation so that I could afford to buy more herbs."

A radio station next told his story, and was inundated with calls. People began flying in from Australia, Germany, and other areas of the world. "The police became regular visitors to my place," he says, "making sure I did not tell anyone the herbs were any good for anything. But I didn't need to say anything. The world was so desperate for something natural that would work that I was constantly running out of herbs."

John Heinerman, a scientist writing in the December 1981 issue of *Health Express,* the journal of the

International Academy of Nutritional Consultants, made a public confession of his original doubts about Jason Winters and his herbaline tea, which he now calls "miraculous." In the article he told about "Jason's terrible problems with the Canadian Protective Health Agency [the equivalent of our FDA] several years ago, when they stormed his house with a search warrant and confiscated all of his herbs and literature," and about the "hardships Jason and his family had to suffer when they fled to Nassau in the Bahamas to continue their work of helping others in the fight against cancer."

Greedy people already had tried to take him over, and had begun harassing Jason even before the raid on his Canadian home. Then friends took up a collection so that he and his family could flee to Nassau and set up a company there. Jason says of that period: "We started receiving over two thousand orders a day, and that has continued with absolutely no advertising. We had to hire all the unemployed people we could find to help us, and still the business grew. Over one thousand letters each month pour in, telling of the relief and cures obtained from all kinds of ills. Hollywood stars, politicians, all types of medical professionals, attorneys, truck drivers, etc., order regularly." Avarice prompted some people to package imitation teas under the pretense that they were the same as the Jason Winters herbal tea formula, but they apparently lack the healing magic.

Jason has an interesting theory to explain why he believes the tea works. "God placed a certain herb in each continent to cure illness by simply purifying the blood," he says. "Life is in the blood, and if anything purifies the blood then a person's God-given natural immunity will have a chance to take over and fight all disease. The herb that God put in Asia will not grow elsewhere, and the same goes for the chaparral of North America and the red clover of Europe. If you try to grow these herbs elsewhere they do not thrive because of soil deficiencies. Jesus spoke of one herb for purifying the blood, Buddha of another, and the North American spirit fathers of yet another. Now, in those days before coffee, white sugar, processed foods and fast-food outlets, any one of these herbs would have done the trick on its own. However, we alive today have such toxic bodies that we don't know what good health really is; after all, we have nothing to judge it by. We're fed on canned milk from birth, then doctored-up cow's milk and canned baby food, graduating to hamburgers, french fries, coffee, and white poisonous sugar. That is why just one of these herbs would not work on me. I was so full of toxins, as we all are, that it took the combined effort of these three most powerful herbs to bring me back to health."

Jason says that on a recent trip to England he was "met with open arms" by the medical profession, including physicians and radiologists who were eager to try his tea. One of them tested himself before and after drinking it, on his radionics machine, and found that it raised his energy level from 47 to 88. He also claimed that the tea worked on the mental and spiritual planes as well as the physical. Startled by this assertion from a highly regarded radionics expert, Jason recalled the words of the old lady in

Singapore: "This herb will bring the spiritual and mental bodies into line with the physical body."

Unlike some of my remarkable new friends, Jason Winters completely accepts the idea that he is a Walk-in, as does his family. "My children are all convinced of the change," he says, "and can readily accept the Walk-in status. So does my wife. It explains so many things that had puzzled us before we came to understand that I was in fact a different person."

The Guides say of the changeover: "Jason Winters was a discouraged, frightened man when he became aware of the future awaiting him without tongue or jawbone, and was not able to face the prospects of such a disastrous operation. During that long biopsy probe, he subconsciously prayed for release from the agony awaiting him, and since it was apparent on this side [the spirit plane] that he would be able to survive no more than a few months after such a drastic operation, another volunteer entered his body and began to revitalize it. This occurs more often than those in physical body realize, for without this reenergizing many such patients would shortly die. The new Jason Winters was an adventuresome, optimistic soul who accepted the challenge and brought back within his awareness the knowledge of ancient herbs that have been known throughout history, but only in isolated areas. By combining those he selected through his inner knowing, he drew into the body the necessary ingredients to rejuvenate the cells and make them slough off the cancerous ones. His optimistic attitude and the reenergized cells provided the necessary stimulus, and thus the rejuvenation occurred."

Jason recalls that after news of his miraculous recovery appeared in some newspapers, he was asked to address a meeting of nutritionists. "I had never spoken in public before," he remembers, "and I was very nervous about it. I made notes of the most important points on four-by-five cards, so that I could refer to them. The night finally came and I started to talk. Suddenly I thought to myself, Hey, this isn't the speech I was going to give. I kept talking, saying things that I had no reason to know. The audience was captivated. I still kept talking, and was as interested in what I was saying as they were. I was startled at my own knowledge, as I went into great detail about the poisons in certain foods that we regularly eat. The response to my lecture was astounding, and I received more offers for more lectures. I never told anyone except my family that this information pouring out of me was originating from somewhere else. It was at this time we realized that I was being used and was no longer my old self.

"I've recently finished two four-hour radio talk-shows in Honolulu, enough to shake the very best professional, but I was able to answer all the questions about herbs, illnesses of every kind, foods, reincarnation, and karma nonstop. Listening to the tapes afterward surprised me, because the answers I gave all proved correct upon checking. I take no credit for any of this, as I know it is not my doing. I know I am being used for a purpose, but I am surprised that 'they' chose a knucklehead like me."

If the former Jason Winters was a "knucklehead," his replacement obviously is not. Jason regularly addresses health-food conventions here and abroad, "and it is here that the miracle proves itself," he says. "People by the hundreds come up to me, grab my hand and start crying. At a recent Long Beach convention nine of them were crying at once. It seems they had all read my story, tried the tea, and become well. I have trouble not weeping myself when confronted with such an outpouring of love. Of course I tell them that God is responsible, and that all I did was follow what Jesus, Buddha, and the others told us to do. I am still overwhelmed by it all. Both my sisters are shocked and astounded by the change in me, as are my relatives in England. When strangers seek me out to ask questions, I am as astonished by my answers as they are."

Most of the Walk-ins whose cases I have studied were in the midst of a marital breakup at the time of the ego transferral or shortly thereafter and have since divorced. After all, it must be quite a shock to find oneself wedded to a stranger. I therefore asked Jason about his marital status, and it was his wife, Jan, who replied: "Before Jay [Jason] had cancer, I was and still am a dominant person, a typical Aries, and Jay was not. Now Jay is as dominant and forceful as I am, and this does make for a lot of sparks between us. However, we are beginning to understand what has happened and we are adjusting. Mind you, it takes work. It is like living with a different person, and that's what he is.

"Jay did not realize that he was now a dominant personality until we had a conversation with our son Alan, who is studying psychology in college, and from out of the mouths of babes came this truth. You mentioned to Jay that some of the other Walk-ins have had a lot of trouble with their marriages, which has led some to divorce. Well, I can understand that, as Jay and I have had some problems, and it is difficult to live with someone who is other than the person you promised 'to love, honor, and cherish.' I am confident that we will be able to work things out, now that we know the problem. When I read your book *Strangers Among Us,* I knew you were talking about someone like Jay. And you know what? I was not surprised. I already knew that I was living with a Walk-in."

Other interesting changes occurred as a result of the substitution of souls. Jason says that although the hospital in Prince George, British Columbia, Canada, definitely diagnosed emphysema, and he found his activities severely restricted, the condition totally disappeared after the biopsy and ego transferral.

Further, although he had been christened Raymond Winters and was called Ray by family and friends, he could not seem to recognize or respond to the name after his awakening from the anesthetic. "I had an overwhelming desire to be known as Jason," he told me, "although I had never previously thought of the name. When I was called Ray it took me several seconds to respond. It was as though it was not me. Ruth, I know this sounds crazy, but the name transition was smooth and easy, with my wife and all our friends calling me Jason or Jay with no trouble at all. It is almost inexplicable, and we still do not understand it. All we know is that Ray Winters underwent the biopsy operation and Jason Winters emerged. Ray was broke, but Jason is now a very successful businessman.

"Over a million and a half people drink the herbal formula each day with results that are truly remarkable. Life is in the blood. Purify the blood and your God-given immunity will take care of any disease. The herbs purify the blood, that's all."

I asked if he really believes that the herbal tea works for everyone, and he replied thoughtfully: "No, I don't think that. Attitude has a great deal to do with it. I have a theory that if you're a jealous, bitter, or uncaring person, you are dumping poisons into your body that nothing can heal. You have to take the herbs with the same love as God gave them to us. You must have faith in yourself as well as in God and His herbs."

An unsolicited letter from Jason's sister, Edna Johnson of Surrey, British Columbia, adds an interesting footnote to the Jason Winters story. In it she said, "I spent a few weeks with him in England last year. In some ways he is the same old Ray, his given name, but he seems to know so much more than I ever remembered! We both had only eight years of schooling in England. Also, he does not remember a few things which ordinarily I should think that he would. Our mother had two items that she was particularly proud of: a very large silver tea-coffee service on prominent display and a granddaughter clock of which we were all very proud. Ray, or rather Jason, didn't even remember them; and I'd mention quite a few things that happened, which he should have recalled, but he didn't. Yet I find him so optimistic, full of life and of knowledge."

Jason's inability to recall some of the objects and

incidents that seem important to members of his family is not surprising. A Walk-in inherits the memory patterns of the Walk-out, but just as we can no longer remember many happenings of our earlier years, so a Walk-in would have even greater difficulty in bringing to mind things of an unimportant nature that had not involved his or her own emotional system. After all, a Walk-in is not the person who lived through those events or shared those possessions.

In completing this chapter on Jason Winters, I asked the Guides if they had any further comments, and they wrote: "Jason will soon develop another process with equally startling results, for his is a far-seeing mind, and his dedication to helping others will make itself felt in the years to come. He will be able to assist those who will listen to develop a natural life-style, free from additives and harmful chemicals, so that abundant good health will lead them toward survival in the difficult years ahead. He is able to recall ancient formulas that have healed in ages past, and to find the ingredients, long forgotten, that were put on the bountiful earth to keep humans free from disease."

I had the pleasure of meeting Jason and Jan Winters in person shortly thereafter, and was exceedingly impressed by the handsome, tall, rugged appearance of this dynamic man, whose exuberant manner bespeaks sparkling health. And just as this manuscript was going to press, I received a letter from Jan saying that "the other morning Jason awakened so excited that he jumped out of bed, exclaiming that he had been given a powerful new formula. He wrote it down, and spent the next few days at libraries reading medical journals. He found that the different ingredients in the formula have been investigated for years by separate medical researchers, yet have never been put together. Separately they proved beneficial in many ways, but Jason's plan to combine these new herbs has been greeted with enthusiasm by everyone to whom he has talked. It will be called Perisel, and people have already started ordering it before it has been manufactured. It looks like a giant breakthrough against degenerative diseases."

Although it is too soon to assess the value of this new product, it would seem that Jason Winters is already beginning to fulfill the Guides' prophecy about him.

CHAPTER II
DICK SUTPHEN

Some twenty-odd years ago, shortly after becoming interested in the psychic field, I read an obscure book by Jack London called *The Star Rover*. It is the fictionalized account of a man sentenced to life imprisonment in solitary confinement who, through self-hypnosis, managed to maintain his sanity by projecting his mind to more pleasant surroundings outside the walls of San Quentin, and to relive some of his own past lives. This was the first time I had heard of astral travel, and in the ensuing years I sometimes found myself wishing that the book could be made a part of every prison library. Surely such a story could bring hope to the incarcerated, I thought, and help "lifers" to keep body, mind, and spirit together by developing similar psychic gifts.

Many years later I met a professional hypnotist named Dick Sutphen, when we appeared jointly on David Susskind's nationally televised program in New York. I instinctively liked Dick, a handsome, blue-eyed six-footer, and was impressed by his abilities when he hypnotically regressed two members of the studio audience to past lives in ancient Rome. By then I had had enough experience with prenatal regressions, both as a subject and as an amateur hypnotist myself, to know that his was an authentic demonstration and not mere stagecraft. As time went by, I accepted several of his invitations to speak at seminars that he and his beautiful dark-haired wife, Trenna, were conducting in Scottsdale, Arizona, but it was not until the summer of 1981 that I learned of Dick's connection with the Jack London book that so long had intrigued me.

By this time, through a series of so-called coincidences, Dick had come to accept that he and Ed Morrell, the western outlaw on whose experiences Jack London had based his prison account, were somehow the same person. But because Morrell died at the age of seventy-eight, eleven years after Dick Sutphen was born in 1937, Dick and Trenna had sought to explain the discrepancy by viewing our past and present lives as "parallels." In other words, they surmised that a soul is capable of experiencing numerous incarnations at once, and that the individual identities superconsciously communicate with and influence each other.

I personally do not believe that, and my Guides

deny it. To me, after hearing Dick's account of his ability to "remember" many of Ed Morrell's experiences, before he had even heard of Morrell and *The Star Rover*, it seemed evident that at some time in the not-too-distant past Ed Morrell had assumed Dick Sutphen's body as a Walk-in. I never place much reliance on my own hunches, however, and it was not until several weeks later that I remembered to consult my Guides about it. On doing so, they wrote:

"As to Dick Sutphen, yes, he was Ed Morrell, who became so eager to return and finish his work and do the writing that he was unable to do before, that when he found a literate, attractive man with enormous potential but little direction who was willing to lay aside his own ambitions until another lifetime, Morrell happily changed places with him, and began with a great burst of energy to create fertile soil for his projects. The original Dick Sutphen is on this side [in spirit] and watching with fascination as the work progresses. He is delighted with the way Morrell is pursuing his goals, and says, 'I'm learning more from watching him than I could ever have learned in that particular lifetime. Good going!'"

At a later session, I asked if the Guides could more definitely pinpoint when the substitution of egos occurred, and they wrote: "It occurred during a traumatic time after a quarrel with his first wife, during the period when he was moving to Arizona. He was in something of a rage, deeply depressed and thoroughly disgusted with the life that he was leading. Ed Morrell took over at the time of deep depression from which Dick was suffering because of his inability to cope with his wife and to understand the direction of his future. He discovered that he felt inadequate in his new surroundings (in Arizona), and during this depressed period the transferral was effected."

Sometime afterward, when I told Dick that the Guides believed him to be the Walk-in of Ed Morrell, he did not seem surprised. I asked if he had any idea when such a transferral of egos might have occurred, and he replied: "If it happened, I should say it would have had to be when my first marriage was breaking up and I was moving to Arizona from the Middle West. I was really depressed at the time, but afterward everything began falling into place."

The original Dick Sutphen, born in Omaha, Nebraska, to a Presbyterian family, had intended to become an artist, and since boyhood had spent most of his free time drawing illustrated cartoons for comic books, instead of playing ball with his friends. He loved reading, too, but the books he chose were invariably about the Dalton gang and other western outlaws.

Immediately after high school graduation, Dick enrolled at the Los Angeles Art Center, and became fascinated with the streets and byways of Hollywood, although at the time he had not heard of Ed Morrell and had no way of knowing that Hollywood was the home of Morrell in his later years. After graduation Dick returned to the Midwest, married, and became an advertising agency art director on such outstanding accounts as General Mills and 3M, while winning top awards in both commercial and fine arts. But his marriage was turning sour, and on vacation he headed for Arizona and the desert, to which he had felt irresistably drawn since visiting it during his school days at the art center in California.

While in the Phoenix area he discovered that fellow artists were finding a creative outlet for their talents in the burgeoning metropolis, and because his wife was agreeable to a divorce he returned home only long enough to sell his art studio and house and turn over their publishing business to her. Then he headed for Scottsdale, on the outskirts of Phoenix, and a new life in the American Southwest.

The Valley of the Sun then, as now, was a teeming cauldron for every type of occult movement, from metaphysical churches to astrologers and trance mediums, but Dick was not interested. He says of this period in his life: "The conflict with my wife had been extremely upsetting. I thought I was in love with another girl in Minnesota, but she was so incapable of making decisions that I finally ended the affair. The art business was not particularly good at this time, and I became exceedingly depressed. Then strange things began happening to me and around me."

One of these occurrences was an eerie encounter with "possession" by a roommate of a girl whom he had occasionally dated. The two girls would play around with a Ouija board from time to time, and while so doing one afternoon in Dick's art studio his friend's roommate suddenly was "possessed" by a male entity, who became dangerously abusive and then tried to jump out of the window. Dick frantically grabbed a telephone directory and began dialing local psychiatrists, but none was willing to come out to treat an unknown patient. "Make an appointment with my secretary Monday," one replied.

Desperate, Dick did what he could to calm the girl and then raced down the street to a white frame house with a sign outside: Chapel of the Golden Dawn. He had heard that a woman professing to be a psychic lived there, and when Rose Figiuola opened the door to his frantic pounding, he quickly poured out the story of what was happening in his studio a block away.

The chance encounter (although psychics say that there is no such thing as chance) changed the direction of his life. Rose Figiuola not only gave him excellent advice for dealing with the immediate situation, but in the following days foretold many specific happenings for Dick, all of which began to come true with surprising rapidity. Baffled by these strange occurrences that were outside the realm of his own knowledge, he began reading in the metaphysical field. One was a book on self-hypnosis, and by following its directions he had an extremely vivid experience of being "lifted out of my body and going far out into space."

He enrolled in evening development classes with Rose Figiuola, and was constantly amazed by her seeming ability to diagnose hidden illnesses and to predict coming events for himself and his classmates. Through Rose he was led to Don Weldon, a Phoenix hypnotist who specialized in past-life regressions to help his clients understand their current hang-ups. After enrolling in his course, Dick discovered that the ability to hypnotize himself and others came naturally to him, and that he could paint his finest pictures while in a self-hypnotic trance.

Upon completing his training under Weldon, Dick launched the Scottsdale Hypnosis Center, and began neglecting his art work in favor of his new hobby. He also developed a unique system of carefully controlled group hypnosis, which is now widely followed by other hypnotists. Trenna Hartman was a student in his classes, and with her marriage foundering she filed for divorce and made a trip to Mexico. Dick went along, hoping that distance from his workaday world could help him assess the strange coincidences that seemed to be giving a new direction to his life; but at the edge of an ancient graveyard in Alamos, Sonora, he became hysterical, and had to be pulled sobbing back to his hotel room, where he deliriously raved about being murdered for "trying to preserve the books."

In subsequent hypnotic regression sessions and sittings with psychics, Dick learned that he was apparently one of the victims of a bloody massacre said to have occurred at that spot four hundred years earlier, when Spanish priests ordered all Indians who refused baptism to be put to death. But at the time of his outburst he nearly frightened Trenna out of her wits. Later that evening, after becoming more calm, he had a vision of Ponderosa pines, and heard a voice whispering, "Go move to the pine-covered mountains just above the desert, for it is there that the tribe is uniting. It is there that your voice shall be heard."

Trenna flew back to Phoenix, and Dick wandered

Mexico for another six weeks, tuning into archaeological ruins and pyramids that seemed familiar to
him, before returning to work. Then he had another
vision of the Ponderosa pines, and felt such inner
prompting that he persuaded Trenna to go exploring with him for an area such as that envisioned.
They found it a hundred miles north of Phoenix,
and within a short time he and Trenna were married
and settling into a mountain home above Prescott at
Groom Creek.

Then came another of those momentous "coincidences" that seemed deliberately intent on leading
Dick Sutphen down new and untrodden paths. He
met David Paladin. David, about whom we will hear
more in the next chapter, is an outstanding Navajo-
Anglo artist who, with his wife Lynda, was living
nearby and enjoying phenomenal success with his
painting, while also teaching art and parapsychology
at Prescott College. Some of his parapsychology students were attending hypnotic group regressions
that Sutphen was conducting in the college yoga
classes, and Paladin sent word that he would like to
meet him. A few days later Dick dropped by David's
studio, and an instant friendship clicked into place.
Each shared the same two overriding interests: art
and the psychic.

During one of their social evenings together the
conversation turned to Mexico, and Sutphen commented on the beauty of Sonora. David responded
that although he agreed about the beauty, he had
had a shattering experience there that took him
quite a while to get over. "Do you know the cemetery
on the edge of town?" he asked reflectively.

Shivering, Dick said that he did, and David continued: "Well, I completely broke down there. I went
to pieces, and they had to literally carry me out of
the place. I saw an old white church on the site, but
there's no such structure there." He said that the services of a local psychic were enlisted by friends to
calm him down, and from her he heard the story of
a supposed massacre there by Spanish priests, who
exterminated the local Indian tribe for resisting con-
version to Christianity. Afterward, she claimed, the
Spanish priests began "dying like flies," and as a
form of exorcism the remaining Spaniards removed
the Indian shrine and placed a Christian cemetery at
the site.

Dick sat on the floor in stunned silence. Not only
had he undergone a similar trauma there, but he
had previously been given a life reading by Kingdon
Brown, an outstanding medium, who said that in an
earlier lifetime in Mexico Dick had belonged to an
Indian tribe that was suddenly wiped out, but that
the reincarnated tribal members were assembling
again in Arizona. Through hypnotic regressions
Dick had already met several who seemingly relived
that horrible experience in Sonora, some as tribes-
men and others as the murdering priests. Now, here
was another member of the tribe that was "assembling in Arizona."

As Dick was now an acknowledged master in the
field of hypnosis, and David Paladin seemed to be a
channel for several discarnates who spoke through
him while in a trancelike state, the two men made
their talents available to each other. Dick was gathering material for a book about reincarnation, and in

one of their taped sessions he asked an entity speaking through Paladin if he (Dick) had ever shared a previous lifetime with a close friend who is a country music writer. The heavily accented voice asked Dick to visualize the friend, and then remarked that although it might not seem so he actually owed that friend a great deal. In a former lifetime, the voice continued, the current music writer was one of those responsible for sending Dick to prison, but through that experience he had met Jack London, who eventually influenced him to become a writer.

Dick was mildly intrigued, but the extent of his follow-up was to ask an author-friend if Jack London had ever been in prison. Yes, he replied, once for lobster poaching and once for vagrancy. A year later, during a chat with Richard Bach, the celebrated author of *Jonathan Livingston Seagull*, Bach suddenly turned to him and asked, "By the way, Dick, have you ever read a book of Jack London's called *The Star Rover*? It's about reincarnation and astral projection . . . about a man in prison."

Dick says that a shiver ran down his spine. With an air of foreboding he asked Bach why he had mentioned the book, about which Dick had never heard. "I don't know," he replied. "It just came in."

Through the help of a friend in California Dick was able to secure a copy of the out-of-print book. He learned that it was the fictionalized story of Ed Morrell, a western outlaw who was sentenced to life imprisonment, much of the time in the San Quentin dungeon where he was forced by a sadistic warden to wear a tortuous "jacket," a contraption that killed most men. Morrell, however, was able to survive the torture by achieving an altered state of consciousness that carried his mind outside the prison to observe living people and to experience past-life situations.

Perhaps the expression, "I was railroaded," originated from this dark period in the opening of the West. In the early 1890s the Southern Pacific Railroad allegedly cheated hundreds of small farmers and ranchers out of their land. With the help of slick lawyers and hired gunmen it dominated the political and economic life of those living in the San Joaquin Valley of California, and when the victims could find no legal redress some of them began holding up Southern Pacific trains, using dynamite to open the baggage cars. An organized group known as the Evans-Suntag gang was among the most active, and Ed Morrell was the youngest member of the twenty-five-man gang. In 1893 he broke Chris Evans, the outlaw leader, out of the Fresno jail, and in doing so disarmed the constable. This was the only charge brought against Morrell when, after seven weeks of hiding out in the Sierra Nevada Mountains with Evans, they were tricked and captured. For this minor infraction of the law in the Wild West, Morrell was convicted in ten minutes by a railroad-dominated jury and sentenced to life imprisonment.

The Star Rover details the unspeakable tortures inflicted on Morrell, whose fictional name was Darrell Standing. Caged alone in a four-by-eight-foot dungeon cell, where he was allowed no reading matter and was fed a scanty meal only once a day, Morrell, fearful that he would lose his mind through lack of human contact, first invented mental games, and then developed self-hypnotic astral projection, so that he could mentally roam outside the prison walls.

Then an even more sadistic warden introduced Morrell to the "jacket," a torture device designed to crush the wearer to death, inch by inch, in unbearable pain. Miraculously, through astral projection, he survived in the "jacket" for nearly five days, and upon being released from its constricting folds collapsed on his straw mat, bleeding and partially paralyzed. During the ensuing week, while he hovered near death, he underwent a psychic experience in which he heard a voice saying, "You have learned the futility of trying to fight off your enemies with hatred. You have seen that your sword of defense was double-edged, cutting deeply into your own vitals rather than overcoming the evil which has been working against you. From today a new life vista will open up and you will fight from a far superior vantage point. Your weapon will henceforth be the sword of love, and as time progresses and your power unfolds, this new weapon will cut and hew away all evil forces that now oppose you." The unearthly voice went on to tell him of his ultimate release, with a pardon from the governor of the state.

The warden, nonplussed that Morrell had not only survived but seemed in good mental health, slapped the battered prisoner back into the "jacket," and under self-hypnosis Morrell began traveling astrally to other jailhouses, inspecting conditions and developing concepts for prison reform. One place to which he was repeatedly drawn was a restful town of fruit and flowers in California, and a schoolroom occupied by students. Most of their faces were blurred, but in his mental travels he was particularly attracted to a girl with clear blue eyes who seemed to be about twelve or thirteen years old.

In these mental wanderings he was also drawn to an older man in Alameda County, whom he followed and watched. Then, one day, the man, whom he instantly recognized, walked into the solitary confinement area and said, "Morrell, I am the new warden." He promptly moved the suffering prisoner to the prison hospital, and after his recovery made him head trusty, over the protests of the prison board. This new warden, Major John W. Tompkins, later told Morrell that he had refused the governor's first request to become prison warden, but discovered after a second call from him that the pencil he idly held in his hand had written "Ed Morrell" on his scratch pad. He called a state official to ask if the name meant anything to him, and upon learning that Morrell was a "dungeon man" at San Quentin, he felt impelled to accept the governor's offer.

Four years later, Morrell was pardoned by Acting Governor Warren R. Porter on Tompkins's recommendation, and almost immediately began lecturing around the country in behalf of prison reform. Jack London, who also had had a personal taste of prison, heard of his story and decided to tell it in a book, but when he discovered that Morrell lacked sufficient education to jot down his memories, he sent a young journalism student to conduct interviews with him. Now grown, she was the youngster to whom Morrell had been drawn in his astral travels to her schoolroom. Eventually they were married.

The Star Rover by Jack London was published in

1915 to indifferent success. Nine years later Mr. and Mrs. Morrell launched a publishing company, with a book called *The 25th Man,* which was a personal account of Ed Morrell's own experiences. They also founded The American Crusaders for the Advancement of the New Era Penology, an organization to initiate prison reform. Morrell is considered the father of the prison honor system, and was called before the U.S. Congress to testify on the subject of prison reform.

What does all of this have to do with Dick Sutphen? For many years before hearing of Ed Morrell, he had been experiencing dreams of hiding out with another man in the mountains. Both were holding lever-action rifles, and when he saw an 1894 Winchester 25/35 lever-action, saddle-ring carbine in an antique shop in the Arizona mountains, he felt impelled to buy it, although he could ill afford it. He hung it above his fireplace, and long afterward learned that it was the same model used by Morrell.

Under hypnosis Dick Sutphen seemingly had been tapping into the Morrell life, and when asked, "Do you write?" he had replied, "I've been trying to write, but I don't know how." This statement seemed contradictory, since Morrell was the published author of *The 25th Man,* but further investigation uncovered the fact that it was Morrell's wife, not the ex-convict, who had written the book for him under his by-line.

Parallels between Ed Morrell and the present-day Dick Sutphen continued to manifest. The moment that Dick was introduced to self-hypnotism he had known exactly how to use it. As a hypnotist he was a natural, skilled at helping subjects to experience their past lives through prenatal regression, and to dip into his own soul memories. Like Morrell, Dick had started his first publishing company without prior experience, but knew instinctively what to do to make it successful. With no background in public speaking, he became a skilled and popular lecturer almost overnight, when his interest shifted from art to psychic phenomena. These were all skills Ed Morrell had painstakingly acquired after fifteen years in the penitentiary.

These parallels seemed to indicate that Morrell had indeed entered Sutphen's body as a Walk-in, but two facts disturbed me. From an early age Dick's reading matter and the childish cartoons that he drew focused on western outlaws. During his youth he had a recurring dream about hiding out with another man in the mountains. If Morrell did not enter Sutphen's body until the breakup of his first marriage, why had he previously had these dreams and these interests?

I posed the question to the Guides, who, after reminding me that the transferral of egos occurred shortly after Dick moved to Arizona, wrote: "It was Morrell who then became active in the psychic movements which had failed to excite much interest in Sutphen. The original Dick had known Morrell in that Wild West life and had helped to hold up a train, but escaped. He hid out for a time in the mountains, but did not repeat his escapade. He liked Morrell and had felt drawn to him, because in two previous lifetimes they had been buddies, one in ancient Mexico at the time of the Indian massacre in

Sonora, and another time in Europe when both had been gentlemen of the Court at Versailles. The elegance and artificiality of that life is what doubtless prompted both of them to seek more adventuresome lives in the raw frontier."

The Guides said that Morrell and Sutphen had both known Trenna in the French lifetime, and again in the last previous one. "The original Dick knew Trenna as his wife in the period when he was a rancher's son in the Southwest and had tried to help hold up a train in revenge for the ill treatment of his father, uncle, and others at the hands of the railroad," they explained. "Morrell in his last lifetime was not at all a bad man. He was an outlaw, yes, but fired with hatred for a railroad that was cheating the helpless people of the West, and until his metamorphosis in prison he was destroying himself through hatred and his wish for revenge. In his enlightened state, after the psychic experience, he brought to fruition the goodness and strength of a noble character, and he did much to pay off any karmic debt through his determination to help others by prison reform. Dick Sutphen, through his admiration for that friend, also benefitted, and brought back with him memories of those days. That is why he felt such nostalgia for the outlaws of the old West, even as a child."

Thus, if the Guides are correct, the circle has come full-turn. Trenna in at least two previous lives knew both Morrell and Sutphen, but in her immediate past life she was the wife of the Dick Sutphen who is now in spirit, and her present husband's body is now occupied by the soul of Ed Morrell. As Alice said while in Wonderland, things were getting curiouser and curiouser.

This wove such a tangled web that I hesitated to pass the new information along to the Sutphens, but in a long-distance phone conversation with Dick I reluctantly read him the passage.

A short time later I had a letter from Dick in which he reported that he had hypnotized Trenna, "and during a lengthy session she totally focused in upon the relationship between her and the 'original' Dick Sutphen's former life at the time of Ed Morrell." He said that the "original" Sutphen, in his immediate past life in the old West had, according to Trenna in her trance state, "robbed a train, was wounded, and gave it all up, but did continue to be an undercover contact for the bandits." He added: "Trenna provided a lot of other details about this, none of which we have yet had a chance to verify, though she certainly agrees with your Guides on the information."

Through research and personal investigation Dick and Trenna have become convinced that Morrell and Sutphen are the same person. So, apparently, does their handsome little son, Travis, who, at the age of three-and-a-half, accompanied them on one of their research trips to the Fresno area of California, where much of the action took place in the Morrell saga. At a restaurant patronized primarily by local cowboys, Travis explained to the customers: "When my daddy was another man he was in jail around here." Dick still remembers the blank stares.

He is also intrigued by the fact that early in his career as a hypnotist, long before he had heard of

Ed Morrell, he began working with life-term prisoners on astral projection with hypnosis tapes.

Meanwhile Dick and Trenna Sutphen are blissfully happy in their marriage and are making a pronounced success of their publishing and lecturing businesses, which grew so rapidly in Prescott that they were forced to move back to Scottsdale to avoid the long commuting distance twice weekly from their isolated mountain home. Dick has authored several books in the field of reincarnation, and their seminars in Arizona and California draw thousands of enrollees from every part of the country. They have now moved their headquarters to Malibu, California, where the climate is more salubrious for Trenna, and where they are enlarging their publishing enterprise.

I asked the Guides for comment on the work that Morrell/Sutphen is accomplishing, and they wrote: "Dick wants all to realize their potential and awaken the slumbering giant within, by utilizing their inner resources and their untapped talents. He is well on his way!"

It is difficult for some of these "special" people to accept the idea that a transition in their identities has occurred, because of the inherited memory patterns of their predecessors and because the concept is new to them. At the conclusion of this chapter I queried Dick Sutphen about it, and he wrote back to me: "In regard to your question, do I believe I am a Walk-in? The evidence certainly seems to support that conclusion . . . and I just about accept it."

CHAPTER III
DAVID PALADIN

This is the remarkable story of an American Indian boy who ran away from his reservation in Arizona, became a stowaway on a ship bound for the Orient, was caught up in World War II, and while still in his teens was captured by the Germans, tortured and starved to death. But instead of going to the Happy Hunting Ground, he eventually awakened from a thirty-months coma to discover that he had somehow acquired the memory patterns of a Russian artist whose death had briefly preceded his own.

I first met David Chethlahe Paladin in 1980 at a seminar conducted by Dr. H. N. Banerjee, a philosopher from India who is a long-time researcher in the field of reincarnation. Dr. Banerjee kindly had sent me a copy of his paperback book, *The Once and Future Life,* in which he summarized Paladin's adventure as an example of reincarnation. Because my Guides declared that Paladin is actually a Walk-in, I was eager to talk with him, and in subsequent interviews have been able to fill in the pieces of his fascinating life story.

David Paladin, the son of a white missionary father and a Navajo Indian mother, grew up on a Navajo reservation at Chinle, Arizona, but spent much of his boyhood running away and being returned to the reservation. Twice he was placed in disciplinary schools for runaways in Oklahoma and California. "But that didn't do any good either," he says with a reminiscent grin. "I was neither a part of the Indian nor the white world. I didn't like to study. I always wanted to soak up all knowledge through osmosis—to know everything about everything. Flowers, for instance: Where they came from, how they grew, everything. I liked to sketch them, but that was not an Indian subject, so it was counterproductive."

He eventually made good his escape, and in San Francisco stowed away on a ship bound for the Far East. Jumping ship in Australia, he bummed around the Admiralty Islands and other areas of the South Pacific until the Japanese attack on Pearl Harbor, at which point he turned himself in at an American outpost. There military officers minutely interrogated him about any Japanese movements he had observed, but when they wanted to draft him into uniform David protested that he was underage.

"Look, you're just a kid," an officer retorted, "but you're in this country illegally, so you'd better do as you are told."

Forcibly returned to the United States, David was given some training in cartography and then shipped to Europe with the Office of Strategic Services, the legendary forerunner of the CIA that was headed by William ("Wild Bill") Donovan. In Germany, while mapping installations behind enemy lines, he was captured wearing a German uniform and thrown into a Nazi prison camp, where he was grilled, beaten, and starved. When the retreating Germans were forced to evacuate the camp, David and his fellow prisoners were left for dead, and the advancing British troops dumped the one hundred and twenty bodies into a railroad car for removal from Germany for burial. Later, while examining the bodies for identification, they noticed a faint stir of life in one of the "dead" and dispatched him to a British field hospital in Vienna, Austria.

David remained in deep coma, and because he had been engaged in a spy mission behind enemy lines when captured, he wore no identification. In appearance he looks more Caucasian than Indian, and because he occasionally mumbled in Russian while doctors sought to fan his spark of life, he was transferred to a refugee hospital for Eastern Europeans. The war was still raging and communications were chaotic, but eventually David's fingerprints were checked out with those of an American who had been listed as "missing in action and presumed dead." Therefore, while still in coma, David was sent to an army transport hospital in Battle Creek, Michi-

gan, where, after two and a half years, he at last regained consciousness. When asked his identity, he
replied without hesitation, "I'm an artist. My name is
Vasili Kandinski." The problem was that his fingerprints tallied with those of David Paladin, and
David had never heard of an artist named Kandinski. Nor had he known any words of Russian until he heard himself speaking the language.

Subsequent research disclosed that the Russian
artist who pioneered in the field of abstract painting
had died in Neuilly, France, in 1944, at the age of
seventy-eight. David, who was born in Arizona on
November 4, 1926, would have been eighteen years
old at the time of Kandinski's death. The exact time
of his own "death" cannot be determined, because of
the confusions of war.

After regaining consciousness, Paladin was suddenly consumed with a desire to paint, and as the
Red Cross made art supplies available at the military
hospital he began to create sweeping abstracts that
soon attracted attention in the art world. Critics who
knew nothing of David's story were excitedly liken-
ing his paintings to those of the late Vasili Kandinski
in both technique and symbology.

While recuperating David also began to play the
piano, and although neither he nor any of his family
members had ever had an art or music lesson, he
suddenly was transposing music and making new arrangements for the hospital's band. His ability was so
outstanding that when the time came for his release
from the hospital, the band master asked him to stay
on in a paid capacity, and was flabbergasted to learn
that David had no musical background whatsoever.

But Vasili Kandinski had taken piano lessons from boyhood and was adept at musical arrangements!

David has had a diverse career since returning to civilian life. For a time he sold shoes, hung venetian blinds, did odd jobs, served as a disc jockey and as a radio announcer to support himself while he painted. He has also become an ordained minister of the Unitarian Church, has conducted classes in American Indian religious perspective for the Iliff School of Theology at the University of Denver, and has taught art and parapsychology at Prescott College in Arizona.

This is the same David Paladin who has only a sixth grade education in an Indian school. Or *is* it the same David Paladin?

The Guides say of him: "When he became a Walk-in he brought with him great awareness of his own past lives, as well as those of some others. He possesses a towering intellect and an insatiable curiosity that he has pruned to a fine sense of loving and caring for others."

Paladin says that for several years after regaining consciousness, he suffered a very real identity crisis. "Strange and very frightening things happened to me," he muses. "Once I met some German tourists in Chicago, and when they mentioned their home-town I began telling them the names of people I knew there, and they knew them, too. Actually, I didn't know anyone in that German town, so I don't know where my information came from. Then a Catholic priest befriended me, and when he referred to the Irish village from which he originally came, I began rattling off the names of people I knew there.

65

I told him it was my village, too, and gave him my name, except that it was an Irish name I gave to myself, and I thought at the time that it was mine. The priest took me into his home because I was penniless, and everything was fine until friends in Ireland to whom he had written about me replied that the person I claimed to be was dead.

"I was not deliberately lying, you understand. At the time I thought I *was* those people, even though in flashes I remembered that my name was David Paladin. I never did anyone any harm. I was actually trying to be helpful when I brought up the names of people I said I knew, but those incidents scared hell out of me. I thought that I was being possessed, and psychiatrists who examined me didn't help much. In desperation I finally came back to Arizona and talked to an Indian medicine man who had known me and my family. He said that I had always been a shaman, that even as a little boy I used to talk to spirits. Working with him helped me to get myself together, but what helped me the most was meeting my present wife, Lynda."

I had learned from Dick Sutphen about the unusually close relationship that exists between David and his attractive young wife, and when I asked David to tell me about her, he replied: "I have a marriage that has provided me with the unconditional love and friendship that so many dream of. Lynda has allowed the flower of my mind to blossom, and has never attempted to manipulate or repress it. I had experienced a less fortunate relationship [a disastrous first marriage, which David charitably calls a learning experience] that has helped me to recognize the value of what I have now. It is Lynda's insatiable curiosity, her sense of wonderment, and her ability to share in my world that allows me the freedom to be, to grow, and to share."

Apparently, after he became a Walk-in, David had subconsciously realized that he must find her. One day he was on a cruise ship in California, saying good-bye to some friends who were sailing for Hawaii, when he felt strangely attracted to a little girl standing on the deck, and snapped a picture of her. For some unfathomable reason he thereafter carried that snapshot in his wallet, year after year. One day a young woman walked into his studio in Sedona, Arizona, to admire his paintings, and David says, "Although I only saw her that one day, I knew!" She said that she was vacationing there with her mother, and when he learned that they were returning the following day to California, he urged her to come and see him again.

Lynda went back to Sedona the following year, and since his first marriage had just ended, he began courting her, despite the nineteen years difference in their ages. Shortly thereafter they were married, and six years later, when Lynda happened across the snapshot of the little girl, she recognized it as herself. She recalled that she had been seeing her grandparents off to Hawaii on the ship that was identified in the photo.

The Paladins moved to Prescott where, as recounted in the previous chapter, their friendship with Dick and Trenna Sutphen began. The first time that Dick hypnotized David, a voice purporting to be that of Kandinski began speaking through him in a thick Russian accent, describing details of his past life, and even supplying the name of his Jewish landlord in Paris, a fact that David could not consciously have known, since the man had changed his name for fear of Nazi reprisals. Kandinski declared that David Paladin had indeed died as a result of beatings and starvation in the German prison camp, but that through shared energy he had brought the body back to life.

During another hypnotic session, Dick regressed David to an earlier lifetime in which he identified himself as Adolphe Adam, a French composer who wrote fourteen ballets, including *Giselle,* and thirty-nine little-known operas. He also identified his beloved wife, Schatzy, in that incarnation as his present wife, Lynda. If David is now the Walk-in of Kandinski, then Adam was a previous incarnation that could explain Kandinski's youthful talent for music, and also the present David Paladin's suddenly awakened knowledge of how to play the piano and transpose music.

At the time of those regressions, David had not heard of Walk-ins, nor had I, but he had devised a possible explanation for the drastic alteration in his talents, personality, and goals. Employing the Emersonian concept of "an intellect doubled upon itself," he elucidates: "I feel that I have been privileged to blend with and to share the energy and love of another consciousness, one that shares unconditionally my own 'being.' When I regained consciousness after the two and a half years of coma I was admittedly confused. I had, it seemed, two sets of information, my own and Kandinski's."

The "two sets of information" would seem to make this a classic example of a Walk-in, inasmuch as the soul entering an adult body automatically inherits the memory pattern of the Walk-out that has been impressed on the physical brain, much as a computer stores a memory.

Paladin says that were it not for his Indian heritage he would have had a more difficult time adjusting to the alteration, "but because of it I merely accepted the fact that during the long period in a coma I had visited with, and shared in the experiences of, those who had passed over." This, of course, could explain how he came to know the names of villagers in Germany and Ireland, and to take for himself, temporarily, the name of an Irishman who had died.

"But frankly, this is an oversimplification," David continues, "as there were periods of disorientation, fears for my sanity, and an inability to center myself. Ultimately, it was the Navajo medicine man who helped me to recognize my 'gift,' and he provided the vehicle for integration and acceptance of self. My goals, interests, and ideals had expanded. It was up to me to focus upon these new aspects of self and decide if and how to use them. I was free to choose my own pathway, to make it one of beauty or one of disaster. I chose the path of 'sharing.'"

If I interpret David correctly, he believes that Paladin and Kandinski work as a duo, and that all souls at a certain level are one. The Guides strenuously deny that both souls are active within the one body. They say of the situation: "David Paladin is now the Walk-in soul of Vasili Kandinski, but because of his previously held theories he is not yet ready to accept the fact that the soul originally inhabiting his body has gone into spirit. He was not one of those who chose to become a Walk-out, but rather one whose body was so depleted that he was unable to keep it alive. But the artist who came into that body when he saw that the Indian lad was to all intents and purposes dead was able to energize it bit by bit, until life again began to flow through and make it work for him. Kandinski had known David in a previous lifetime in Hungary, where they had been friends and fellow seekers of wisdom through a deep study of psychology. David was also an artist of sorts, and in his next incarnation he chose the vehicle of an Indian on a reservation in order to test the theory that Indians attract strong protectors in the spirit plane, and themselves become protectors of other souls."

This coincides with my Guides' assertion in *A World Beyond* that we can earn the right to choose, between lives, the circumstances of our next incarnation. Many mediums and psychics cherish the belief that Indians are a particularly psychic race, and that each of us has a personal Indian Guide in the spirit plane. They do not, however, explain how there are enough Indian Guides to go around for all of us.

The Guides, in continuing their discussion of the Paladin case, wrote: "When through abuse and starvation David felt himself unable to survive, it was easy for him subconsciously to allow his former friend [Kandinski] to slip into the Indian body that he was vacating, and try to make it work for him. It eventually did work, and because of the closeness of their former ties through several incarnations, the spirit of David sometimes speaks through the friend who now occupies his former body. There is a close kinship, and because of their previous experiments together in the philosophical and psychological fields they do often seem a duo. The 'spirit' David also sometimes brings in another former associate to speak through the artist, but is careful not to interfere with his friend's life or his painting, as he has enormous respect for his artistic talent."

Paladin, under his tribal name, Chethlahe, is widely recognized as one of the foremost Indian artists in the world today, although his paintings are not in the Indian tradition. Rather, they are constantly evolving abstracts in the manner of Kandinski, whose own talent seems to be progressing smoothly.

I asked the Guides why, if Paladin is actually Kandinski, other personalities sometimes speak through him, and why he receives a great deal of material through automatic writing. They replied: "Paladin is open to several entities who are permitted to communicate through him, just as we write through you with your permission. There is, however, only one entity in his body, and that is Kandinski. He is a fine man of superior intellect and talents, and is interested in helping mankind. Otherwise he would not have been permitted [by enlightened souls in the spirit plane] to revive and enter the body that had been occupied by another. His wife is a loving, caring, delightful woman who helps him exceedingly, and has known him well in several previous lifetimes."

I pressed for more details about David's previous lives, and the Guides declared: "He was at one time a Buddhist monk, and at another time an artist of considerable renown in the Far East. He was also a musician in a previous earth life before he was the Russian artist who now occupies the body of Paladin. David errs in thinking that the original ego is still occupying that body, for although the previous David is taking a keen interest in the progress of his successor, the Indian boy of yore is not the occupant. The other voices that occasionally manifest through him result from his attainments, in previous lifetimes, of contacting strong spirit guides who still manifest through him from time to time. When he became a Walk-in he brought with him great awareness of his own past lives, as well as those of some others whom he had contacted while in coma."

David espouses an interesting theory: that rather than incarnating in lifetime after lifetime, we continue to exist as separate entities, but thereafter can explore our potentials through a simultaneous merging with a variety of different individuals who are in physical bodies. When I queried the Guides about this, they responded: "The theory is an old one that he held in the previous lifetime as Kandinski, but it is not correct. The Walk-in phenomenon was not generally recognized at that time, as fewer were coming in then than now, when the tempo has been enormously stepped-up because of the approaching shift of the earth on its axis. The true explanation of reincarnation and Walk-ins is that which we have al-

ready given you. Paladin/Kandinski is there now to
smooth the way for others through his love of mankind, and to open their minds to the potential in
each of us for soul advancement in flesh as well as
spirit. A fine, fine man, and one with enormous potential for good."

Because I have immense respect both for Paladin
and the Sutphens, the latter two of whom were influenced by the former's beliefs to accept the theory of
"parallel lives" as an explanation for reincarnation, I
did not want to be in the position of contradicting
them. Each of us has a right to develop his own precepts, and none of us at our present stage of development is in a position to prove the others wrong.
I therefore questioned the Guides closely about their
own "theory," and in their usual didactic way, they
asserted:

"The theory of parallel lives is unsupportable. We
are one ego from the beginning of our creation as a
spark showered off from the Creator, until the end
of time. We have natural affinities for others of
those sparks with whom we have shared many lifetimes on Mother Earth, and we react with and to
them in ways that bind us together or set us apart
from them, but there is only one I, one You, one
separate soul as far as our earth lives go. When a
Walk-in replaces one who leaves, he is thereafter in
sole charge of that particular human body. The
other retires into spirit, where he will naturally be
interested in the progress of the one who now bears
his earthly name and his relationships, but it is not a
sharing in the sense that both egos are active in that
body simultaneously, or by taking turns. Walk-ins do

not become Walk-outs, because that would violate their pledge and the purpose for which they returned to earthly life, but as in the case of David, he sometimes makes his functions available for a discarnate to speak through him. David's one-time body is now occupied by the soul who, in his most recent incarnation, was named Kandinski. The entity who, for playful reasons, uses a Russian accent in speaking through Paladin, and who is nicknamed Kandi by Paladin's fascinated friends, is actually David Number One, who, from the spirit plane, is supplying information and guidance to his successor."

After completing this chapter on David Paladin, I asked him to read it and make any comments he chose. He courteously replied that if he were to add anything to it, it would be this: "Humankind has long been enchanted with the concept of 'absolute truth.' Indeed, because of our very nature we seek the safe harbor, one from which we can venture forth and explore, reassured in the knowledge that there is something, someplace we can depend upon. Truth, however, constantly evolves. The safe harbors give way to forces of nature and Becoming. Our own perspectives or that of our Guides provide 'truths' in order that we can become safe explorers, and in exploring, discover that the creative process that we call God is growing, changing, and exploring with us and through us.

"Ruth and her Guides and I may appear to hold separate truths, to be venturing forth from different harbors. Yet we know in our hearts that we are one, exploring together the wonderment of Becoming."

I also asked my old friend Dr. Albert Hugh T.

Doss, a practicing psychiatrist in Raleigh, North Carolina, for his comments, knowing that he had met and talked with David Paladin. My friendship with Dr. Doss goes back more than thirty years, when we dined together at the beautiful home of his family in Cairo, Egypt, which has since become an embassy. At that time I was a syndicated columnist, and on my assignments in Egypt was being assisted by Albert's brother, Maher Doss, who was a press attaché in Egypt's Foreign Office. Maher had graciously invited me to his family's home, and afterward Albert, a young Cairo physician, drove me to some archaeological digs then in progress near the pyramids of Giza. We had lost track of each other for a quarter-century until Albert, reading that I was to be a speaker at a David Sutphen seminar in Phoenix, made the long trip there to renew our acquaintanceship. Unfortunately I was ill and unable to attend, but because life moves in mysterious paths, it was there that Dr. Doss met David Paladin, and as a psychiatrist became interested in his case.

Dr. Doss and his delightful wife, Madge, recently visited with us in Washington, and after their return to Raleigh he wrote to me as follows: "I have just reread *Strangers Among Us* and have been fascinated by its logic. The concept of Walk-ins seems to fit in with the cosmic pattern that when great crises or changes affecting the earth and all mankind are impending, illumined entities come from the One Creative Source to help mankind. Man is not ready for the shift of the earth on its axis, soon to take place, and the political, economic, and moral breakdowns now occurring. Man, in his great ignorance, needs 'enlightened beings who can forego the time-consuming process of birth and childhood, returning directly to adult bodies,' as you said in *Strangers Among Us.*

"I met David Paladin and his wife Lynda at the Sutphen seminar in Phoenix and felt a warm sense of rapport with him as he told me the story of his life. At that time I had no understanding of the Walk-in concept. Since reading *Strangers Among Us* I have become more enlightened and can state with conviction that in my opinion David Paladin is an excellent example of a Walk-in. He manifests all of the characteristics of a Walk-in."

After summarizing the known facts about his transferral of egos, Dr. Doss wrote: "David continues to be aware of his own previous personality as he grew up on the Indian reservation, and this also conforms to the concept of a Walk-in. He is familiar with, and has not lost what he had acquired in his personality, talents, and interests before his so-called 'death.' In 1978 David founded an organization known as the Foundation for Noetic Synthesis, to promote a holistic understanding of man through publications, seminars, workshops and research programs. What better endeavor could a Walk-in, Kandinski, occupying the body of David Paladin, have than this? To my mind it emphasizes the credibility of the concept that David Paladin is a Walk-in. After considering all the known facts, I am convinced that David Paladin is, indeed, a startling example of a Walk-in."

Dr. Doss then made this interesting observation: "In my practice of psychiatry I must occasionally deal with persons who are potentially suicidal. In your book you have pointed out a new and valuable approach to this real and often critical problem. After all the suggestions and techniques normally used by my profession have been tried, the psychiatrist might discuss with the patient the possibility of allowing his body to be occupied by a superior (in spiritual understanding) being. This being would be allowed to solve the insurmountable problems (as viewed by the patient) and also to carry on his own expression in a life of service to mankind. The patient would be encouraged to keep his body, the temple of the soul, in excellent condition, without drugs or a self-inflicted mortal wound, so that it would be ready for the incoming Walk-in. He would simply vacate his body during peaceful sleep. After all, in this time of organ transplants, is it not reasonable that when a person feels that he cannot solve his problems on the physical plane, he could allow a Walk-in to occupy this body and use it to accomplish good for humanity?"

David Chethlahe Paladin, since finding "himself" following the death experience, is indeed contributing to the betterment of humanity, as he lectures, paints, and conducts seminars and workshops at his present studio in Albuquerque, New Mexico. And as I complete this chapter I note that New York's Guggenheim Museum has organized a massive exhibition featuring "the pioneer abstract painter Vasili Kandinski." Thomas M. Messer, director of the Guggenheim, remarks in the show's catalogue that Kandinski is "the patron saint" of the gallery, which owns one hundred and thirty of his works, more than of any other artist.

CHAPTER IV
ELIZABETH NACHMAN

I had never heard of the Association for Spiritual Development and Research (ASD&R) nor of a psychic called Elizabeth, when a man who introduced himself as Leslie Nachman telephoned long distance to ask me to be a speaker at the ASD&R's month-long series of seminars in Horseshoe Bend, Arkansas. For that matter, I had never heard of Horseshoe Bend, and when I learned that the only way to reach it was by private plane from Memphis or through winding country roads for several hours after exiting from Interstate 55, I politely declined, saying, "I don't like to fly in small planes."

"Then we'll meet you by car at the Memphis airport, and drive you here," he encouraged.

"But I hate long automobile drives," I pleaded.

"So do we." I could almost hear him grin, as he added: "That's why we fly our own plane. We can bring you in for your speech each Wednesday, or we'd love to have you stay the entire time and enjoy the facilities. It's a spa, you know."

When I explained that I could not possibly make four such grueling trips, or be away from home for an entire month with a husband and little dog to "manage," Nachman countered, "Bring them along. We'd love to have them."

As I do with most speaking invitations, I declined. But by the next morning some inner prompting had caused me to reverse my stand, and in May 1981 Bob and I, with our Maltese dog, Muffy, drove cross-country for three days from Washington, D.C., to Horseshoe Bend. I had by then learned that the founder-president of ASD&R was the psychic known as Elizabeth, and that other speakers would include my long-time friends Dr. Stanley Krippner, an internationally respected parapsychologist; Dr. Ishwar C. Sharma, an author and professor of philosophy from India; and Dr. Gina Cerminara, a well-known author whose book *Many Mansions* helped project Edgar Cayce into the national spotlight.

Other lecturers would include Dr. J. Allen Hynek, director of the Center for UFO Studies and former astronomical consultant to the U.S. Air Force; and Bernard Gittelson, consultant and lecturer who computerized the science of biorhythm and has served in an advisory capacity to the West German government and the European Common Market. Obviously a high-level assemblage of talent!

On our arrival at the Hillhigh Lodge in Horseshoe Bend, where the seminars were being held, we were welcomed by two officers of the ASD&R, who, while showing us to our room, asked eagerly, "Is Elizabeth a Walk-in?"

Realizing from the question that they had read *Strangers Among Us,* I laughingly exclaimed, "But I haven't even met her. I don't know anything about her."

"You'll see!" one of them said, and the other added, "She meets all the qualifications. She's totally devoted to helping others."

The first week's seminar was already in progress, and the mysterious-sounding Elizabeth was so busily engaged with it that I did not meet her until that evening, in the association's crowded little office off the hotel lobby. After my earlier hesitation about accepting the invitation, I was pleased to observe that she was slim and attractive, garbed in a tailored slack suit rather than a witch's flowing black cape. And no broomstick!

We settled down for a get-acquainted chat, and I was comfortably listening to the soft cadence of her well-modulated voice when suddenly, for only the second time in my life, I distinctly saw a human aura. The first occurrence had been several years earlier, when, during a lecture by a Central American psychic, he was all at once surrounded by a bright green halo, which I could not dissolve even when I closed my eyes or shifted my gaze to a blank white wall and then back to him.

Now, in this crowded little office with its overflowing ashtrays and littered wastepaper baskets, I saw a brilliant golden aura completely encircling as much of Elizabeth as I could see above the desk behind which she sat. And the aura continued its illumination throughout the remainder of our conversation.

I was so exhilarated by this strange (for me) occurrence that, although I had recently been neglecting the automatic writing, I slipped into the vacant office early the next morning, before the lobby was astir with people, and asked the Guides to tell me whatever they could about Elizabeth. Then, after my brief meditation in the darkened room, they wrote on the borrowed typewriter:

"She is one of the most superior people alive today. A saint who has returned with full knowledge of her mission in life. She is a Walk-in, but the one who began in that form was also a fine soul who was preparing the way for another to return to physical body. Elizabeth is on a higher plane than most, and in a previous life was an Ascended Master. We are sending our special blessing to all those who are participating there, and also to Les [Nachman], a remarkable and somewhat unrecognized person who came into this lifetime to assist in the noble work of the one called Elizabeth. His present mission is as important in its way as hers, because without him the functioning and development of that exceptional ability of Elizabeth's would be less perfect."

Only later did I learn that although Elizabeth seldom uses a last name, it is actually Nachman; and that although their eleven-year marriage ended in divorce in 1975, she and Les both work full time without pay for the ASD&R charitable foundation. I still knew little about this association, except that it owned a large farm where the Nachmans were raising cattle and produce, to teach others how to prepare for the difficult years ahead, but when I asked the Guides for more detail, they wrote:

"As we said yesterday, Elizabeth is one of the highest Initiates, as they are termed in India. In many lifetimes she devoted herself to the good of others, forsaking riches for the richness of the inner life. She and Les were together in a Roman incarnation when he was a senator and she a high priestess who uplifted the tone of the debauched court. They fell in love and she left her priestly duties to be with him, but in the exaltation of their love she so influenced him that he in turn left the Senate, with all of its privileges and power, to join her in the temple. They have had their ups and downs, but in recurring lifetimes they seem to find each other in one or another relationship. Not in every earth life, but in many! Their work together now is vital to the next few decades, when many will be brought to the realization that scarcity of food and natural disasters are marking the close of the Piscean Age. They will cluster about these two for sustenance both of the spirit and the physical body, and as they emerge in roles of leadership for a wide area of the land, more and more will come to view them as the rescuers they will be. Here they are depositing the seed that will grow and develop into a pattern for all America and spread its tentacles beyond the seas. Let them take heart in the knowledge that although obstacles will often be encountered, these will be met and overcome, and their efforts will come to fruition. God smiles on them."

Reading this message afterward, I thought that I had seldom known the Guides to heap such lyrical praise on anyone. No wonder they had apparently jogged me to change my mind and come to this remote area in the foothills of the Ozark Mountains! Yet, in a subsequent session with the Guides, they hinted that I might have been powerless to resist the speaking invitation. "Ruth," they wrote at a following session, "you and Elizabeth were closely associated in that Persian life of which we have earlier told you [in *Companions Along the Way*], when Edgar Cayce was there too, as Uhjltd, the doctor-priest at the City in the Hills and the Plains," near present-day Schustar, Iran.

"That is not the last lifetime in which you have known Elizabeth, but the ties are so strong that when Les asked you to come and you were saying no, the Forces stepped in to reverse that decision. Your inner awareness recognized those age-old ties, and here at Horseshoe Bend you felt instinctively, from the first moment of meeting, that Elizabeth was almost a part of yourself."

It is true that I had felt an instant liking for Elizabeth, and that I was nearly overwhelmed by her aura, but was she in fact a Walk-in? So many at the seminar were by now asking me that question, and Elizabeth herself seemed so sure that she was *not* a Walk-in, that I finally approached her ex-husband about it. Did he believe that the woman to whom he was formerly married was a Walk-in?

Without hesitation, the not-always-approachable

Leslie Nachman replied, "I can tell you the exact day, the hour, and almost the minute when she became one. But I won't talk about it unless I have her permission." And with that he wheeled about, and strode away.

Elizabeth was so totally preoccupied with the seminars, her lectures, and individual counseling that for three weeks she could find no time for an interview. Then we talked at length, and since she freely gave permission for Les to speak of his own views, I was able to piece together her story.

Elizabeth Serles Nachman is blonde, svelte, and attractive, with the lissome figure of a fashion model, which she once was. Born into a professional family in southern California during the 1930s, she occasionally demonstrated psychic abilities as a child, and during her college years at the University of California at Los Angeles proved to be an apt subject for psychic experiments conducted by her professor of psychology.

Her first marriage was a disaster. Accustomed to a peaceful home presided over by gentle, soft-spoken parents, she found herself embroiled with an intolerant husband who had no patience with her or their three small children, and they lived together only eighteen months in all, during the five years' duration of their unhappy marriage.

Compelled to make a living for herself and her children, Elizabeth entered the business world, and at the zenith of her career owned seven flourishing dress shops in southern California, including one in fashionable Beverly Hills, and she also manufactured clothes under the Liz Roberts label. By then she had acquired a mansion surrounded by twelve acres of land adjoining that of actor James Cagney's in the exclusive Cold Water Canyon section of Beverly Hills.

Elizabeth had definitely "arrived" by the time she met Leslie Nachman, a successful Hollywood booking agent and entrepreneur, who came into her Beverly Hills store one day to purchase a mink coat for his current girl friend. It was certainly not love at first sight. In fact, for a time there was some animosity between them, but Elizabeth's children adored Les, and after the marriage he gave them the father's love they had heretofore lacked.

Before long they sold their California interests and moved to Florida to be near Leslie's ailing mother, buying a mansion on Palm Tree Drive in Miami Beach. Les bought a car rental firm and expanded it to include boat rentals, and Elizabeth became Elizabeth Arden's general manager for all of her high-fashion shops in Florida. Les Nachman, a native of Brooklyn, New York, who had been president of his local boys' club, and a song-and-dance lad in school plays, now added a music publishing company to his holdings, and everything that he touched seemed to turn to gold. He was living a charmed life: rich, successful, with a beautiful wife and a ready-made family of three children on whom he lavished fatherly affection.

Then tragedy struck, although like a fog it crept in softly "on little cat feet." Elizabeth's seventeen-year-old son Jim had been nominated by Representative Claude Pepper for the Air Force Academy, and had easily passed the rigid physical examination, but before he could take up the appointment he awakened one morning feeling decidedly unwell. A doctor diagnosed the trouble as typhoid fever and sent him to the hospital, where within a few weeks his six-feet-two-inch, 180-pound frame had shrunk to 120 pounds. At the hospital the diagnosis kept changing, finally being labeled "an unknown virus," and during the two and a half years of his catastrophic illness Jim underwent fourteen major surgical operations, the shortest of which lasted nine hours. During one of these his colon was removed and his duodenum accidentally perforated. Peritonitis set in, with raging fever. For the remaining eighteen months of Jim's life he existed solely on life-support equipment, in an intensive-care unit. His veins broke down because of the prolonged intravenous feeding, and his weight plummeted to seventy pounds. In all except mental capacity, he had become a vegetable.

Between her anxious visits to the hospital, Elizabeth had meanwhile studied and been ordained as a minister, and was filling their house with destitute refugees whom Les was always stumbling into in their upstairs bedrooms and bathrooms. To avoid marital friction they therefore bought the old twenty-one-room Hertz mansion on Indian Creek, to house Elizabeth's indigents and to serve as her offices.

Jim's condition continued to worsen, and his mother was in agony. On Christmas night in 1974, unable to sleep, Elizabeth wandered into the library where she felt the urge to pick up a pencil at the desk. Immediately it sprang to life, and apparently began bringing her a telepathic message from her dying son, who begged her to release him from his pain-wracked body. "It's not me lying in that bed," the message said in part. "We all must die. You know that, so let's start there. I want to die. Mother, please let me just go home. I can't stand any more, and it has to be better there than here. Let me go. Don't cry. Mother, all the things you tried to teach me I now know. Please, Mother, listen and let me help you through your mental pain. Let me tell you what it is like. You were right. God is good. I'm able to see where I am going now, and I am not afraid. There are many people waiting to welcome me, but I can't leave you with those tears. Help me, Mother. Let me go. Let me go, please. Let me go. It is beautiful, and music like that I have never heard."

Musing about that sad night in retrospect, Elizabeth says: "It was as if Jim were talking to me. Apparently in his unconscious state he was communicating psychically with me. But although many were urging me to give permission to cut off Jim's life-sustaining equipment, I could not do it. He was a vegetable physically, but not intellectually."

The dying young man sometimes engaged in spirited debates on current events with his mother. At other times he slipped into a trance state, seemingly reliving a past life during World War II when he had been an unwilling guinea pig for doctors in Nazi Germany. He would call Elizabeth by a different name during those periods, and would hold long conversations with her in German, although in his waking state he did not know that language. At other times, speaking English, he would cry out that the doctor who was now treating him was the same

German physician who had "cut me up before, and now I'm his victim again." When the doctor walked into his hospital room Jim would freeze, beg that he be prevented from approaching him, and refuse to take any medicine that he prescribed.

During this traumatic period Elizabeth was still trying to perform her duties as a counseling minister and caring for her waifs and strays, while virtually going without sleep and barely taking food. Les saw her wasting away before his eyes, as she endlessly traveled back and forth to the hospital to lavish her love on a dying son whom she could not bring herself to release.

In July 1975, fully aware that she was being grossly unfair to her husband, both emotionally and financially, she called their attorney and said, "I want to free Les. Please draw up divorce papers."

Nachman, appraised of her action, said that he did not want to be "free," but Elizabeth insisted that he move out of the house and "resume a normal life." Knowing that he also loved Jim deeply, she explained: "I can talk about it, but you can't. You must have a life of your own. This is my responsibility, but there's no reason why everyone else should be destroyed."

Les reluctantly moved to an apartment, and the divorce proceedings began. By the end of August Elizabeth had been spending her nights in Jim's hospital room for six weeks, and Les occasionally saw her there when he made his daily calls on his stepson. He sensed that only her nervous energy was keeping her alive. Then, at the beginning of September, a mutual friend telephoned Les to say that something was drastically wrong with Elizabeth. He rushed to the house and found her staring vacantly into space, unaware of her surroundings. Les summoned a doctor-and-wife medical team who were personal friends, and after taking Elizabeth to the hospital they tried to give her sedation, but she kept resisting them, saying, "I don't want to go to sleep. Jim is going to die."

Finally they took her back home, where she at last fell into a deep sleep, and since she had almost no discernible pulse the doctors remained throughout the night, monitoring her failing life signs. In the morning her daughter took over the bedside vigil, and after sleeping for thirty-six hours Elizabeth suddenly awakened. Asked how she felt, she replied: "What do you mean, 'How do I feel?' I feel fine! I'm going to pull the plugs."

Les Nachman says of the transformation: "She looked five years younger. Even the shape of her face and head seemed altered. That day she gave the order to disconnect the life-sustaining equipment, and within two or three days Jim passed peacefully into spirit. Elizabeth didn't even cry. She had exhibited a paroxysm of grief several years earlier when a friend died, but now she was calm and resolute. She had a new sureness and serenity. We went through the funeral together, but she was an entirely new personality. Afterward, even her sense of humor was changed. The things that we used to laugh about together weren't funny to her anymore. I didn't know this new woman."

My Guides say that during Elizabeth's thirty-six-hour coma, at a brief moment when the monitoring doctors could find no heartbeat, the original occupant of that body passed into spirit. She knew that her son should be released, but she could only make that decision if she went with him. She chose to leave, and at that point another entity, highly energized and eager to help mankind, slipped into the body and sensibly made the decision to pull the plugs and free Jim from his futile suffering.

Les and the new Elizabeth continued to live apart, but were friends, and when the divorce decree became final that fall she established a charitable foundation, deeding to it the two mansions, their automobiles, and whatever else had survived Jim's catastrophic medical bills, which amounted to more than $400,000.

"Elizabeth consulted me about it first," Les says, "and I told her to do what she wanted to. I had turned everything over to her in the divorce settlement. I'd always been able to make a good living, and I was still young enough at thirty-nine to start over again . . . or so I thought. A friend and I went into business with a machine that could improve one's golf stroke, but it didn't improve my finances. I tried other business ventures, but since the divorce from Elizabeth nothing seemed to go right for me."

I asked Elizabeth for comment on her transformation after the long coma, and she said: "I suddenly knew exactly what I wanted to do with my life. My surviving two children were now established, and I wanted nothing for myself. They raised no objections whatsoever when I told them that I wanted to give everything away and devote the rest of my life to helping others help themselves. I set up the association, and one of our first actions was to start a Helping Hands program, to ease the burden of those who were caught in a temporary financial bind."

The foundation launched a weekly television show, syndicated to several Florida cities, titled *A Psychic Called Elizabeth,* on which she counseled those in trouble and raised money to assist abused children, battered wives, and those like herself who had suffered financial disaster through catastrophic illnesses in their family. The program became so popular that lawyers, dentists, doctors, and business people donated their services to assist the tragic victims whose cases Elizabeth discussed on the air.

"When a family was facing financial ruin because of some unexpected catastrophe we would see that the mortgage, or rent, and the utilities were paid while they waited for insurance or government checks," Elizabeth explains. "Our volunteers helped them to fill out the necessary forms. The fund-raising we did on television and radio was a bridge over troubled waters, a means of preserving human dignity for the unfortunates. We supplemented the income of a poor girl who gave birth to twins, sending her a hundred dollars a month, and she never knew where the money came from. A cooperating dentist made new front teeth for a battered mother of two small children, whose husband had struck her a shattering blow in the mouth. A lawyer volunteered to help her file charges, and we found her a job. Another dentist provided new teeth for four children who were badly smashed up in an automobile accident. All of these professional people donated their services without charge."

The new Elizabeth was extremely intuitive, and with her awareness and psychic attunement she became highly sought after as a private counselor. She was donating all her time and energy to the foundation, taking no salary, and having her counseling fees paid directly to the association, which had fifteen hundred members, but only two or three hundred who actually paid dues. Although reared in a Methodist family, Elizabeth was being led deeper and deeper into the psychic field, as a healer and teacher, and Florida police began calling on her to help solve baffling crimes or to locate missing children.

With her acute sensitivity, Elizabeth realized that mankind was facing dire prospects for the next two decades, before the shift of the earth on its axis and the dawn of a new age in the twenty-first century. She felt an intuitive need to establish a community in a safe area of America, where those who wished could set up separate households and learn survivor skills, experience spiritual growth, and look out for one another.

Explaining her vision for the community, Elizabeth said: "We can't just intellectualize. We must become doers and use our talents—physical, mental and educational—to prepare for the troubled times ahead. I wanted a retreat, a shelter where we could educate people to improve their body, mind, and spirit, to be healthy and learn to carry their own weight. A place where, if war or famine strikes, others can flee from stricken areas to find a haven with us."

The project existed only in her mind, until a stranger walked into her office one day and offered to sell 520 acres of land in an economically depressed area near Salem, Arkansas. Elizabeth did not know the region but in a psychic flash she knew that "this was it," and that it was a safe area. She agreed to buy it sight unseen, and after conferring with fellow officers of the foundation, arranged to sell the Miami Beach mansions in order to make the down payment. Then she dialed Les Nachman.

Reminiscing about that quixotic telephone call, Les says: "Elizabeth began the conversation by saying, 'Les, I need you for a project. There won't be any money to pay you—nothing but hard work. Will you help me?' She then told me of her dream to establish a refuge on a farm that could eventually feed a lot of hungry people. If she had asked me a few months earlier, I would have turned her down. I would not have agreed to do it for the former Elizabeth, but I was now dealing with a new person, who was not my former wife. Her influence over me had become much greater. There was no longer the old hostility. This new woman had no physical attraction for me, but I admired her tremendously and believed in her. I said I would help, and before long I had wound down all my business activities and was doing hard manual labor on an Arkansas farm, clearing forest land and digging post holes."

Among his other skills, Les is a licensed pilot, and borrowing a friend's plane they flew up from Florida to inspect the already-purchased property and buy 320 acres that adjoined it. Shortly afterward the foundation leased 400 additional acres that were partially irrigated and contained five catfish ponds. Then they moved to Arkansas and started working like field hands. When the land was sufficiently cleared they began acquiring Hereford calves for fattening, and some of the foundation members individually bought calves that the farm cared for and fed. Each was tagged with the owner's name, and at market time the proceeds were split fifty-fifty, or the butchered meat equally divided between the owner and the foundation.

Members of the association began visiting the farm, and because of their trust in Elizabeth's psychic judgment some of them gave up their Florida residences and bought small houses or condominiums in surrounding towns like Salem and Horseshoe Bend. Elizabeth conducted Sunday services and reactivated the Helping Hands program to assist needy people in the economically depressed area. The foundation stocked the ponds with 100,000 catfish to be raised commercially, and on learning that a local hatchery was culling baby chicks, bought a hundred for ten cents apiece. These chickens, unlike those in commercial hatcheries, were allowed to scratch on the ground and roost normally, and since they were fryers rather than layers, when the time came to kill and freeze them Elizabeth made a festival of it. Three knowledgeable foundation members taught the others how to singe, pluck, and dress the fowl, and after the onerous task was completed they picnicked together. They also began raising turkeys, and thereafter each Thanksgiving Day is celebrated on the farm like the original one in Massachusetts, with members gathering on a beautiful knoll overlooking the lake, to give thanks and to feast on the produce from the farm.

To meet the mortgage payments Elizabeth must still travel frequently to New York, California, Florida, and other areas where she gives psychic counseling to foundation members and celebrities. Between trips she lectures, teaches, and works in the fields, pitching hay and driving tractors alongside Les and the two paid employees, one of whom tends the catfish ponds and the other the cattle.

In the early summer of 1980 the Nachmans looked on the land and found it good. But suddenly one morning they discovered to their horror that during the night an infestation of worms had invaded the hayfields and was rapidly destroying the year's crop. Elizabeth fled to the telephone and called her son Dennis, a biologist and genetics researcher in California. After she had frantically described the worms, he said, "I'm sorry, Mom, but the entire hay crop will be gone within twenty-four to forty-eight hours. There's nothing you can do in that isolated place to prevent it."

Sick at heart, she returned to the fields, and while she was relating the disastrous news the sky turned black. In another moment an enormous cloud of blackbirds swooped down into the fields, and within a few hours had eaten every worm. The crop was saved!

Then came the drought, seriously affecting all of Arkansas and the surrounding states. Without water for their crops, farmers were forced to unload their cattle at a tremendous loss, but the foundation reaped enough hay to feed all of its cattle and sell the remainder to neighbors. The foundation also sells beef, catfish, poultry, and eggs to the members at cost, and donates them to those unable to pay.

It is unfortunately true that the world is inhabited by far more takers than givers, and some members take advantage of the Nachman's generosity, for without Elizabeth's donated counseling fees and Leslie's hard work there could be no foundation. A few of those who moved to the area to become a part of the endeavor have drifted away, and no one tries to stop them. Some take the free handouts, but are "too busy" when it is time to chop firewood, work in the hayfields, dress and freeze chickens, or work in the thrift shop.

Such stalwarts as Arthur Frohock, and Martha Severin and Elsa Strassweg, two retired librarians, are shining examples of volunteerism, and the association could use more like them. If there are others who would like to join the community, I can testify that it is as far removed from a cult as any society could be. No one is coerced into doing anything or told what to believe. People can go and come as they please. There is no communal living, and without the inspiration and the drudgery of Elizabeth and Leslie Nachman the enterprise would doubtless collapse. Their ideals and dedication are the mainstay, and through their influence the association has attracted to its seminars a variety of internationally known speakers on a wide range of New Age subjects.

I recently saw Elizabeth again in California, where she was launching a three-hour call-in show every Sunday evening on a Los Angeles radio station. The program is shortly to be syndicated around the country, and will sometimes originate by remote control from Salem, Arkansas, when commuting is difficult. During our visit together I asked Elizabeth whether she now believes herself to be a Walk-in.

"I accept it completely," she replied. "A number of things have occurred recently which make it obvious to me that I am not the same person who was born into this body. For instance, I had not been back to southern California for a number of years, until a few months ago. Through my brother I met some friends of his who asked me out to their house. I spent several hours there, and when I returned to my brother's house, he asked, 'What do you think of the old neighborhood?' I replied that since I'd never been familiar with that particular neighborhood, I gave it no particular thought. My brother was stunned. 'But Elizabeth,' he exclaimed, 'you and your first husband lived three doors away from there for several years. It was the first house you bought, and your daughter was born there!' It was my turn to be stunned. My brother drove me back out there, and pointed to the house where I had lived during that marriage, but it seemed only vaguely familiar. I had no sense of having once occupied that house.

"Another curious thing occurred during that visit. My brother said he had mentioned to an old friend of mine that I was coming, and that she could hardly wait to see me. He spoke her name, and I had no recollection of her. My mother could not understand it. She said, 'But Elizabeth, you would *have* to remember her. She was your closest friend all through junior high school. You two girls used to drive me crazy, because you were so inseparable. You were like the Bobbsey Twins, who had to be together every minute.' Yet I don't remember her, and it was the same with others my brother mentioned, including one he said had been a steady boyfriend of mine."

This lapse is not surprising, because although a Walk-in inherits the memory patterns implanted in the physical brain of the body, the incidents involving emotions cease to have meaning for the successor, and often cannot be brought to surface recall.

Friends of Elizabeth's have commented on another curious phenomenon. In speaking of her surviving son and daughter, to whom she is devoted, she always refers to them as "these children," or "the children." She was unaware that she never says "my children." I asked her about this, when it was called to my attention, and she said, "But we have a friendship relationship! I don't really think of them as belonging to me. They're just wonderful people."

This new Elizabeth has an uncanny ability to dip into the future, and many of her publicized predictions have already come to pass, including the strange sinkholes in various parts of Florida. She foresees a time in the not-too-distant future when survival for the many will depend on the few who have learned to utilize their latent talents, acquired new skills, and turned back to the land in cooperative living. She is trying to motivate others by setting an example, and to watch this fragile, city-bred, blonde dynamo pitching hay and driving a tractor is a lesson for all of us. We could nearly all do it if we tried, although most of us would not look that good in blue jeans!

CHAPTER V
BJÖRN ÖRTENHEIM

Despite my growing acquaintanceship with a broad spectrum of Walk-ins, I have met only one who is said to be the returned soul of a world-famous genius of the immediate past.

In the early fall of 1980 Björn Örtenheim wrote to me from his native Sweden, introducing himself as a scientist-inventor who is working on a "cosmic-force receiver" to provide an energy source that will create no pollution and will also heal diseases. Björn said that his American-born wife had recently introduced him to my writings, which excited him because in recent years he has been visited during sleep by "a group of entities of a very high philosophical and scientific nature" who were giving him "information about how to build alternative energy systems." As a result, he added, he has "been able successfully to create a worldwide patented essential function for energy saving in these systems.

"The information that I have received in these vivid dreams contains almost all the details," he wrote, "making it rather easy for me with my technical knowledge to design and build a kind of receiving device to make it possible for us on earth today to utilize different kinds of cosmic forces for healing, and to create all the necessary energy for our home and industrial needs from a clean and natural source."

This letter could have been shrugged off as just another high-flown scheme by a would-be inventor, except for the material enclosed with it: a highly laudatory article about Björn Örtenheim in a glossy-paper magazine called *Sweden Now,* another write-up in a Newsweek publication called *New Products and Processes* that displayed pictures of his electrical vehicles, and enthusiastic letters of recommendation from the National Swedish Board for Technical Development, top-ranking scientists at Uppsala University (the oldest and most famous university in Sweden), and from executives of Paramount and Columbia Pictures. Along with these were certified proofs of grants he has received totaling more than a million and a half Swedish crowns, and a personal inventor-award of fifty thousand Swedish crowns.

This, then, did not sound like a Rube Goldberg comic strip character, and inasmuch as his letter described some technical aspects in the developing of clean energy that were beyond my comprehension, I forwarded it to my Walk-in friend Michael, about whom I wrote at length in *Strangers Among Us*.

Michael, of course, had no personal acquaintance-ship with a Swedish inventor named Björn Ör-tenheim, but within a few days he wrote me to say, "Björn is a Walk-in. The soul now occupying his body is that of Albert Einstein. Ask your Guides."

Actually I had already done so, since mailing off the material to Michael, and the Guides wrote: "Björn is the Walk-in soul of Albert Einstein."

Needless to say, I was electrified by the seeming verification of identity from two such out-of-this-world sources. My Guides, of course, are in the spirit state between physical lives, whereas Michael's super-conscious knowledge comes to him from what he terms Group Mind, and is available to him as a mem-ber, through many lifetimes, of an Inner Brother-hood that has been operative through eons of time. Several years ago, when I was preparing to write about Michael, I asked that he be more specific about this mysterious source, and he replied:

"When an Inner Brotherhood has been in exis-tence long enough, with sufficient members who are strongly committed and dedicated to the goal of helping mankind, a Group Mind gradually forms. This mind then becomes a concensus of all the knowledge and experience of its members, each of whom can draw on it through mental telepathy. Group Mind is something you cannot make happen. It is something that grows from the living mental vibrations and energies of beings who are dedicated to an evolutionary goal or purpose that will give benefit to all sentient beings. Over the ages, as members of these Inner Brotherhoods work and strive and live toward that goal of helping all mankind, the Group Mind forms and grows in strength; but it can only be used in serving and helping others. It cannot be used for selfish purposes, or that member will be denied access to it."

Thrilled at the possibility of being in touch with the returned soul of Albert Einstein, whose remarkable work in the field of physics has revolutionized world thought, I wrote to Björn Örtenheim about the comments of Michael and my Guides, asking if it made any sense to him. If so, could he suggest when the alteration of personalities occurred? Björn replied that the information did indeed make sense to him, and that the transferral of egos apparently occurred in 1967 during an exceedingly traumatic interlude in his life. He said that he and his wife, Angela, were flying to California, where he had some research work to complete, and that they would be stopping by Washington, D.C., to file for a patent for his solar-magnetic-field energy project. They would be glad to call on me at that time. I eagerly awaited their visit the following month, and through our many conversations and subsequent letters have put together his story.

The original Björn was an adventurous playboy, who flew aerobatics in mountainous terrains for the thrill of the game, enjoyed driving fast sports cars, and sailing in dangerous waters. He was a graduate engineer, skilled and efficient, but became bored with office routine and forsook his profession to become the publicity director for Columbia Pictures in Sweden. During this period, to publicize the release of a film called *The Long Ships,* Björn arranged for a Viking ship and crew, with himself as skipper, to sail from Oslo to Stockholm. Many said it could not be done, and the trip proved to be such a rough adventure that it received the greatest newspaper and magazine publicity ever accorded a movie in Sweden, winning for him first prize in Columbia Pictures' worldwide sales and publicity drive of 1964. This occurred three years before he became a Walkin.

From early childhood Björn had a deep interest in technical things. At the age of eight he independently constructed a small sailing boat from plywood, with a sheet as the sail, and launched sailing expeditions in it around Stockholm's inner archipelago of the Baltic Sea. While in junior high school during World War II, he and the son of the Iranian ambassador to Sweden started a biweekly technical magazine called *The Wing,* which carried detailed specifications and pictures of the latest Axis and Allied airplanes, as well as information about their military armament and performance. Björn was trilingual, speaking English and German as well as Swedish, and during the war nearly every foreign embassy in Stockholm subscribed to the magazine put out by a couple of teenagers on a hand-operated off-set printer in the Örtenheim attic.

One day the commanding general of the Swedish air force summoned Björn to his headquarters, looked at him sternly, and demanded: "Where the hell do you get all this information about the military planes of these fighting nations?" Sweden, of course, was a neutral power, and when Björn honestly replied that he simply walked around to the embassies and talked to their military attachés, the general laughed so hard that he nearly fell out of his swivel desk-chair. "Don't you kids know that a lot of spies all over the world are risking their lives for this very information?" he finally asked.

"Well," Björn replied reasonably, "why don't they just subscribe to our magazine instead?"

The general took a liking to the brash, intelligent lad and often took him along on flying trips to inspect Swedish air force bases and troops. Through this friendship Björn eventually joined the air force, and at the age of eighteen became a pilot, but later resigned his commission to return to college, where he received two engineering degrees, in electronics and airplane technique. He then worked with the development group of the Swedish supersonic fighter plane called *The Dragon,* but found the office routine so dull that he went to work for Columbia Pictures, and later for Paramount Pictures.

Meanwhile he had married a beautiful Swedish girl from a wealthy industrial family, whose widowed mother persuaded him to go to work as vice-president of the family concern, because she had no son to take over the helm. Their temperaments immediately clashed, as did their ideas on how to run an industrial empire. To make matters worse, Björn's wife invariably sided with her domineering mother, and he developed a serious allergy that was accentuated by the nervous tension. He therefore resigned his position and took his wife to Spain to make a new beginning, but his mother-in-law followed them there, and more clashes ensued.

They all returned to Sweden, and after a particularly unpleasant quarrel with his wife and mother-in-law, Björn loaded his shotgun and walked down to a deserted beach of the North Atlantic near his home. Ordinarily a sensitive, warmhearted person, he was so upset by his inability to live harmoniously with the two women that he had determined to end his life.

"The winds at that beach are ferocious," Björn mused, as he mentally recreated the scene. "The waves were lashing the shore, and in my utter loneliness my thoughts turned to a friend who had mysteriously died a short time before. He was Dr. Henry Kjellson, a famous Swedish writer with a Ph.D. in technology, who spent ten years with the Dalai Lama in Tibet, and a lifetime studying old Sanscrit writings and the Pyramid of Cheops. In the mid-1960s Dr. Kjellson said that he had solved the secret of the underground chamber of the Pyramid of Cheops, and when leaving Stockholm to return to Egypt he suddenly died at the airport from a severe attack of ileus. Until that moment he was perfectly healthy, and his son, who is a medical doctor, was with him. The son said that as a physician he had never encountered such a strange and unexpected death. A short time later he gave me some of Dr. Kjellson's unpublished material about highly scientific knowledge of the pyramids and lost civilizations, because he felt that I was the right person to continue where his father left off."

The diversion of his thoughts from his own crushing heartbreak to the work of his friend apparently saved Björn from suicide, because he now recalls: "The sound of the ocean's pounding waves and the roaring of the winds seemed to have a hypnotic effect on me, and put me to sleep. The sleep turned into a very real dream in which my body was moving weightlessly in space, entirely disconnected from earth life. I had the feeling that I was being approached in some way by very powerful personalities from outer space, and suddenly my whole being seemed filled with extraterrestrial power. When I awakened I felt incredibly strong and independent. The next day I sold my shotgun, and then the rest of my properties. I irrevocably gave up my connection with the family company, left my wife and her mother, and began intensive study of Dr. Kjellson's fantastic material."

A few days later Björn was visited unexpectedly by two lamas from Tibet. "The lamas simply entered my house without previous arrangement," he recalls, "and conveyed an invitation from the Dalai Lama to visit a Tibetan community deep in a forest of Sweden, where a group of Tibetans personally chosen by the Dalai Lama were studying medicine. The men wore long orange robes, and had shaved heads and bare feet. The barefoot women were dressed in heavily embroidered togas. They greeted me with their palms together and their fingertips touching the Third Eye. Then they bowed and touched my shoulders with one hand, and their hearts with the other. My mother was with me, and she remembers that she had to eat a 'sacred powder' before the meal of Tibetan dishes. Since Dr. Kjellson had spent many years in Tibet with the Dalai Lama, it was as if he were reaching across space to direct my path."

The transference of egos, which Björn believes occurred during that hypnotic sleep in 1967 during a howling windstorm, has drastically altered his direction and his goals. He soon became aware that he was being instructed during sleep by a group of spirits who, because of Björn's technological expertise, could work effectively through him to develop clean energy sources that would obviate the necessity for oil, whose dwindling supply could lead us into World War III.

I asked the Guides about Björn's nightly excursions during sleep, and they replied: "The soul of Einstein lives now in Björn's body. He is in direct contact with highly developed soul sources in the galaxy, and because of his performances in past lives he is given every assistance to speed the rediscovery of forms of energy that will revolutionize the world in the twenty-first century."

After the transition Björn, feeling that he had been neglecting his technical knowledge, moved to the university town of Uppsala to work on his doctoral thesis, and during his research discovered the energy recouping system, now patented throughout the world, which became the inspiration for his electrical vehicles that are currently being produced in Sweden and India. The university meanwhile arranged a grant for him to develop a number of alternative energy systems, such as wind-power plants, solar energy devices, and units producing fresh water from salt water by the use of solar power.

In the mid-1970s he worked closely for a time on

the problems of energy and pollution with the state of California, and it was while there that he met his present wife, Angela, who moved with him to Sweden, where other grants awaited. An official of Uppsala University says of him: "Björn Örtenheim is a researcher and inventor of alternative energy systems. Electrical vehicles of his design and his patented system, automatically recouping about thirty percent of the used energy, are already in production and marketed by large corporations in both Sweden and the Far East. Örtenheim's latest invention, a new method of using solar energy for dissociating water into hydrogen and oxygen for efficient use for driving vehicles in city traffic without pollution, as well as heating, is now being developed and is being supported by research grants from the Swedish National Board of Technical Development."

During this explosive period of creativity, Björn and his wife, Angela, also wrote, produced, and filmed a television documentary about mankind and its energy problems called *There Is a Sunrise Every Morning,* which has been shown as a TV-movie on one hundred forty stations worldwide, and to many high schools and universities around the globe.

Björn is extremely modest about his inventive genius and the international publicity that has come his way. "I made these discoveries, yes," he admits, "but only with the help of Power of Light, which I did not realize at the time I was working on my energy recouping system."

And who or what is Power of Light? When I first met the Örtenheims in December 1980, Björn did not know the answer, but he was aware of the group working with him during sleep, and of a leader who played a predominant role in the instructions. In his reply to my first letter telling him that the Guides and Michael had both identified him as the Walk-in of Einstein, he wrote back:

"There are three strange things I would like to mention to you. Firstly, my previous letter to you was written in a place that has the strongest vibrations I have ever felt. It is a hundred-year-old windmill converted to a summer house, located on the island of Gotland, next to a deserted beach where Angel and I can pick up fossils of plants and animals over four hundred million years old. It was here that I received the information on how to build the solar energy system.

"Secondly, I was encouraged by my wife, Angel, to try to ask the leader of the group of my friends who he was, and why he had contacted me. In a powerful dream the next night in the old windmill, where the secrets of the solar and magnetic field energies were revealed to me, he said, without being prompted, that we were friends working together in science far back in time, in a faraway galaxy. Another member of the group, who reminds me of the Polynesian race, told me that we were working with science in a highly developed civilization that vanished from earth some fifty thousand years ago. This was presumably Lemuria, in the Pacific ocean.

"Thirdly, the other night I was seriously commended to study a certain relationship between my energy concept and Einstein's unfinished theory about gravitation and cosmic magnetic fields. I did that, and a fantastic thing occurred to me. The principle in my concept that has been approved by a professor at the University of Uppsala is that the sun's rays can release a certain energy in a magnetic field, and that a third new power is created that is stronger than the magnetic field. In Einstein's unified field theory he tried to prove, before his death, that the earth's gravitation is not gravitation, but a local form in the universal magnetic field. This is what I will prove if I can develop my solar-magnetic-field energy project."

I had asked Björn to comment on any changes that he noticed within himself after the night of his near-suicide and transition, and he wrote of himself in the third person: "The new Björn does not want to go hunting and kill animals anymore, and even the most frightening guard dogs walk up to him and lick his hand. He is more serious and careful in his speech. He is absolutely honest in his relationships and far less interested in material things. The new Björn has no desire to be a millionaire, only to earn a sufficient living to accomplish his mission and support his family. But he still shares some interests with the old Björn: flying, sailing, music, horseback riding, and wilderness trekking."

After their visit with us, Björn and Angela flew to California, where he was to engage in work connected with his solar energy project. He soon discovered, however, that he was adversely affected by atmospheric conditions there, and he telephoned me several times to report despairingly that his contacts with his group of spirit friends seemed clouded and less clear. He and Angela made a trip to the Grand

Canyon area in the hope that the higher altitude and cleaner air would reestablish clear contact, but that too was unrewarding.

Then, on the night of January 18, 1981, he had a vision, which he described to me in a letter: "My friend's image appeared above me. Just there, and seemingly not for any specific reason. I recognized him from my previous dreams. I finally conjured up enough nerve to ask him his name, and he replied, 'Just call me Power of Light.' That gave me something to contemplate! Then I asked him how I was going to manage this difficult project that could mean so much for mankind. 'It's so big!' I complained. He answered softly, 'Well, you're a pilot, aren't you? We gave you the most powerful energy ship ever given to mankind. You know how to fly it. If you get lost, call the Tower.'"

While briefly in Mexico, Björn again experienced difficulty in making contact with Power of Light, but when they returned to Sweden in February 1981 it was brilliantly reestablished. Exuberantly, Björn wrote to tell me that, and to ask if my Guides could give the identity of his powerful "friend." I relayed the question, and the Guides wrote: "Seraphim or Serapis is another name for Power of Light. He is the archangel directing the force of light transformed from darkness in the European area of the earth, and that is why Björn has difficulty in America receiving from him. The vibrations are weaker for Serapis in the American hemisphere than in Europe. Serapis has had deep influence on many Europeans, including the composers Franz Liszt and Johann Sebastian Bach."

I also asked the Guides about Angela Örtenheim, and they wrote: "She is a highly developed soul who chose in this lifetime to be born into a rather trying situation and has taken on the awesome task of becoming helpmate to a genius, who since becoming a Walk-in is soaring to great heights. It is a task that requires patience, love, and understanding, and Angela is responding exceedingly well. It is not always easy to put another's interests above one's own, but she is well advised to continue doing this for a time, as the rewards will be many. Björn will achieve worldwide attention, and he has great powers for good. Björn will be provided by Serapis with the protection to further his work. He will need to guard against avaricious people who would like to take over his advancements in science, but Serapis will surely alert him to the dangers of certain people through their vibrations, which are so different from those of Björn's."

Several interesting developments occurred after I forwarded these messages to the Örtenheims. He wrote that they had moved their experimental workshop, office, and residence from Marsta to a new location in Sweden on a large seaside plot overlooking the archipelago. "POL (as he now began calling Power of Light) says that the vibrations are much stronger here, and there are less disturbances. On this plot is a small, towerlike building on a cliff overlooking the Baltic Sea, and from it we can see twenty-three islands with forests and rocky beaches. We feel a very strong vibration from POL in this building, and we occasionally go there to receive messages. POL tells me that this little peninsula was

113

the residence of Balder, who became a God of Light according to old Norse tales, and there are still remains from ancient castles. Incidentally, it is interesting that we could rent this place for almost nothing."

Björn enclosed a stereo recording of Bach's Toccata und Fugue in F Major on organ, and in explanation wrote: "You probably know that the Great Pyramid of Cheops is a huge mathematical formula telling most of the scientific secrets from the lost civilizations of Atlantis and Lemuria, and even of the Mayans. If you meditate on a picture of the Great Pyramid, while listening to this recording of Bach's, you may, after a few times, see how the Great Pyramid was built. This music from Bach contains the same mathematical vibration-formula that was used when building that pyramid. The vibration of every tone multiplied through the harmonies in this particular Bach music corresponds with all the mathematical measurements in the Great Pyramid. A computer could easily prove this. If a computer separated the frequencies of every tone in this music and turned these frequencies into numbers, the computer could reveal a perfect replica of the mathematical pattern that shapes the Great Pyramid."

Being neither mathematically inclined nor particularly musical, I can only pass that challenge along to my readers.

Björn seemed excited at hearing from the Guides about Power of Light, writing: "After your Guides told me that POL had a shape on earth as Serapis, we studied an interesting book by Manly P. Hall, *The Secret Teachings of All Ages,* and learned that Serapis was the supreme diety of the sun and that Osiris was the personification of the sun. Also, POL occasionally talks about his Sister of Light, and I assume that this means the Egyptian goddess Isis."

This sounded rather nonsensical to me, but the Guides told me in so many words not to knock it. "Those ancient gods were actual people who once lived in the flesh," they declared. "They were superior beings who through enormous dedication to the Creator and His creations had come to be so revered in ancient Egypt that, after their demise, they were worshipped. Power of Light, as Serapis, was a soaring entity who, having lived for others in many incarnations, no longer needs to return to physical body, but is so concerned about the destructiveness now endangering earth's very existence that he is working through Björn to help avert needless tragedy."

They then asserted that in a previous incarnation eons ago Anwar Sadat, the late president of Egypt, was the same soul who, after his death, was worshipped as the god Horus, and who, during his most recent lifetime as Sadat, was a Walk-in. I eagerly pressed for more details, but the Guides advised me to leave that subject for future discussion.

"As to Power of Light, he is one of a stellar group that has for some time been observing and monitoring Earth people," they continued. "He is able to contact Björn freely because the latter was one of that same group or brotherhood in ages past. The spirit of Einstein lives in Björn, and they are as one in that they were both embodiments of the same spirit that has roamed freely between planetary realms. Einstein was not always an earthling, but a star rover in the sense that he was not wedded to any particular planetary sphere. Björn will soon have the necessary means to begin his pilot plant to produce a form of energy which is new to earthlings in recorded history, but well known in Lemurian and Atlantean times, when he lived there."

From time to time I could bask in the knowledge that I was in touch with such exalted personages, but then would be thrown into a fit of frustration by more letters from Björn, enclosing still more messages from Power of Light that were nearly all beyond my limited comprehension. I have no knowledge of physics, electricity, electrons, and a universal magnetic field, yet Power of Light was pushing me, through Björn, to write about them.

Sometimes I was even caught in the middle between Björn and my Walk-in friend Michael. To cite an example, which may mean something to my readers but absolutely nothing to me, Björn wrote that Michael had sent him two formulas as a test, and he commented to me: "He probably wants me to explain the energy formula that Einstein never had a chance to reveal before his death, which is $E = MC^4$. This is the ultimate energy source and exists everywhere within the universal magnetic field [UMF] as activated materia in a plasma form beyond the speed of light. Energy cannot be destroyed, nor can it be used up. It can only be converted into another form of energy. Everything is energy! Matter is a form of energy, and when accelerated into the speed of light it is converted into another form of energy that is light. However, in certain frequencies of the UMF matter can be accelerated into the ultimate energy form, which can be called super plasma. The super plasma form of energy is a higher dimension of energy expressed in the mathematical formula $E = MC^4$. The speed of light is not the ultimate speed in this or any other universe. All matter is formed by certain patterns of atoms, and the orders of these patterns are forming all the different matter. When converted into the plasma form of energy, the patterns of matter are put out of order and the atoms start running wild at a very high temperature. In the ultimate form of energy, the super plasma, the atoms are continuously expanding at a continuously accelerating speed powered by the universal magnetic field. Our universe is such a form of energy, but the increasing distance between the atoms (our planets and stars) is slowly decreasing the temperature until it finally stops. Our universe is like a form of matter inside the First Universe. It will soon be possible to harness just debris of this ultimate energy form, preferably in the matter of hydrogen, which burns with a pure flame creating only heat and water; and since water contains hydrogen it is recycling itself forever—the pure energy given to us by the Creator that does not pollute our environment. The new formula of the ultimate energy shall therefore be $E = MC^4$, instead of the earlier known and proven formula $E = MC^2$. This new formula may sound like Greek to you, so please ask your Guides what this could mean for mankind if we can harness and utilize this energy source."

I decided that I had troubles enough without engaging the Guides in that discussion, and was grateful that Björn did not press it. But in his next letter he described, in equally baffling terms to me, his designs for a prototype power plant he hopes to build soon that could stop pollution and replace the need for oil. "Power of Light is feeding me information for the hydrogen project at an increasing tempo," he continued, and he enclosed pictures of an outdoor test that he and an Uppsala professor had conducted to "release the energy in a very small amount of hydrogen. We just want to use parts of the energy and transform the hydrogen into a liquid that can be used in the gasoline tanks of cars. We already have the carburetors here so that we can convert our present cars to be driven on hydrogen. I hope you understand how interesting and important this project could be if we can easily and cheaply transform water into hydrogen gas, put it into the gas tank, and drive around. Once the energy in hydrogen has been used, what comes out of the car's exhaust pipe is water and steam, creating no pollution whatsoever. It goes back into water, so what we have is an eternal energy source that does not pollute and frees us from dependency on oil cartels and crisis-politics."

Even I am capable of realizing the importance of such a development as that. But Björn lost me again, as his letter continued: "Last night POL told me that American astronomers recently discovered a so-far-unknown-to-man galaxy ten billion light-years away from the earth. There is the Quasar 3C273, an enormous energy plasma presently expanding faster than ten times the speed of light, radiating energy from the First Universe into our universe, powered by the ultimate force of energy in the universal magnetic field. The ultimate force of energy is created when the UMF is accelerating matter into plasma and then the super plasma form, approaching the speed of light to the fourth power (C^4). This means that this dimension of energy is an extension of the theory of relativity because it is changing continuously in the acceleration and time.

"The reason why the American astronomers could suddenly discover this is because it is from the galaxy where Power of Light and the other powers are fueling the universal magnetic field into our universe ... the power field that is the source of all life and movement of materia in our universe. This electromagnetic field is also carrying all thoughts at immediate speed to the entire universe at the same time. Power of Light and his group think it is now time that they should make themselves known, in order to give hope to mankind on earth. The time has come to let man understand that there are powers unbelievably more powerful than this world's narrow leaders, with their doomsday nuclear weapons. From now on there will be an explosive expansion of human groups powered by universal spirits to reach a higher consciousness, in order to be ready to build a new golden age here on earth.

"Because of their increasing consciousness of the importance of life continuing on earth after cataclysms, POL and his group are now starting to feed important scientists and high-level humanitarians information about their existence. They are feeding these scientists with the awareness that this enormous power cannot have been created out of thin air, and many of these scientists are now beginning to accept the same picture of religion that Einstein declared before his death, when he was wrongly accused of being an atheist. A consciousness accelerating much faster by the increased knowledge received from these different forms of spirits will make it possible for most of these groups to survive the shift of the earth on its axis and create the new golden age."

Björn, who originally had forbidden me to reveal his true identity in this book, said Power of Light had now declared that this was permissible, provided I made clear that it was my Guides and Michael who first informed me that Björn and Einstein were one soul. He said POL feels that the book should be written, because it could give new hope to discouraged earth-people by telling them "about the help that is being brought to them, partly from outer space through the Power of Light's spiritual hot line to advanced souls on earth, and partly from the enlightened Walk-ins who are rapidly returning to earth to seek out those who are looking for a new way of life, to love and share and clean up earth's environment."

POL reportedly told Björn that the first time Einstein appeared on earth it was as a scientist in Lemuria. Between that time and his birth as Einstein he had lived numerous other earth lives and inhabited other galaxies, and he continued: "Einstein tried to teach the people how to use nuclear power and acquire a better understanding of the universe, but his work was betrayed by men who built nuclear warheads that now threaten all life on earth. Einstein had tried to explain the ultimate energy source of the universe in his unified field theory, the secret of the universal magnetic field that is the ultimate source and power for all transmission of light. The movement of all the smallest parts of the atom are also powered by this magnetic field and can be utilized on earth as a clean, unlimited energy supply, but this knowledge is being misused. Einstein died a very disappointed man, and his soul returned to his original power source beyond the Andromeda galaxy. He came back as a Walk-in in 1967 because he felt that he had a debt to repay to humanity, for being a part of the creation of the nuclear bomb. The universal magnetic field is energy, and the energy is, and is controlled by, the Creator."

One day Björn sent me a color slide of what appears to be a UFO that he had photographed in Sweden. Declaring that for some time he seems to have been attracting these mysterious objects, he wrote: "I am hereby sending you a picture to show you what an extraterrestrial UFO looks like and how it is powered by the magnetic field. The spiral antenna on the top is absorbing or taking in the power field from the universal magnetic field (UMF), and from the bottom it is radiating out a different polarity in order to repel the magnetic field of earth. In this way the UFOs can hover, accelerate away from the earth, or descend.

"It is very interesting to see how this field is pulsing all the time. This shows that the pulses of the magnetic field have different lengths, and the length of the pulses are maneuvering the power of the field, making the ship accelerate, stand by, or hover. It is the length of the pulses between the magnetic field that is controlling the maneuverability of this flying object. The pulsing light on top and under the spaceship is ionized air from the earth's atmosphere when the ship is entering it. The air is ionized into negative and positive ions from the ship's magnetic force field powered by the UMF (Einstein's unified field theory), and the ship is maneuvering by balancing between the universal force field and the earth's magnetic force field. You can clearly see the force field like an aura on this color slide.

"If we can create a magnetic power field in a flying object or machine, this power could be pulsing, creating its own magnetic power field, and it could then do all the things mentioned above, by using the earth's magnetic power field as a propulsion and power source. This is the way UFOs are flying in space. We have seen them many times here, but I am informed that most of these flying objects from outer space have not been manned. They are remote-controlled with robots, and are coming here to look at the development on earth, taking measurements of our atmospheric temperature and levels of various chemicals in the air, and making other checks. When we now discover this magnetic power field on earth we are close to reaching the ultimate energy source. One way is to utilize the enormous energy that is stored in hydrogen, and since earth and most of the universe contain hydrogen, it is a source of energy that will never run out. When we learn how to utilize the magnetic power field around the earth we can fly without jet engines, rockets, or propellers. We could just repel the magnetic field in the flying machine against the earth's magnetic field, accelerating out into space or into orbit like a satellite, and land on the other side of the earth in an hour or so."

Although I assume that many of my readers will be as baffled as I am by this technical discussion, I feel that it is important to include the information here, because I frequently receive letters from scientists and engineers who have read my books in the psychic field, and have been intrigued by some of the material.

Björn's next letter enclosed another color slide showing the result of the successful project by himself and his professor-friend to release magnetic/light energy in the open air. "We are releasing the same type of energy that is radiated from the quasars," he wrote jubilantly, "but, of course, on a much smaller scale. The colors turning from blue to red show the hydrogen nucleus released and then broken in the UMF, transforming its moving energy $E = MC^4$ into a new light/magnetic field. The picture shows magnetic/light fusion with water burning and releasing contents of energy from hydrogen, the cleanest and most powerful energy in the universe. When this energy is released and transformed into a useful energy form, the only exhaust that comes out immediately transforms into pure water."

The colors were brilliant, but the picture itself made about as much sense to me as Björn's technical comments. What a pity, I thought, that he was wasting all this time on me, who could understand scarcely a jot of it. Then I goofed again! I politely thanked him by mail for the picture of the hydrogen explosion, and he quickly responded: "The color slide I sent you about our hydrogen project is *not* showing an explosion!!! [The exclamation points were his.] A hydrogen explosion is very simple to create!

What the picture is showing is a continuous fire of burning water, utilizing the ultimate and only clean energy stored in hydrogen and oxygen in water. Forty percent of this entire universe contains hydrogen, and our sun is radiating the kind of energy that we are revealing in this project."

I stood corrected.

By this time Björn was receiving a steady stream of messages from the one whom he calls Power of Light, and POL was repeatedly using the phrase "The closer you work with nature, the closer you work with the Creator." In one message he declared, "Life comes from nature, and the souls from the vibrations of the Creator, transmitted in the cosmic forces. If man destroys either one of the forms of the Creator he destroys himself. If an earth-destroying cataclysm is to be prevented, man has to halt his present destructive course of raping nature, polluting the waters and atmosphere, poisoning the food, building destructive devices, obliterating the forests, and manipulating genetic patterns."

POL agrees with my Guides that a third world war can be prevented, although the chances of doing so are lessening at a frightening pace. They also agree that the shift of the earth on its axis is inevitable near the close of this century, and that it is a necessary process to cleanse the earth of its man-made pollution and of the greedy souls who are trying to manipulate others to their own advantage.

My Guides have thus far declined to delineate the actual shift, but POL has told Björn that it will approximate twenty-five to thirty degrees. He says of that awesome event: "The wobbling of the planet earth is proof that the planet is approaching the moment of the shift, which will take place within a matter of six hours when the time comes. During that time enormous climatic changes will occur. You need only look back to the last such shift when giant elephants in Siberia and North America froze to death within seconds while grazing on flowers and green vegetation. The undigested vegetation is still found in their stomachs, and modern scientists have successfully eaten their meat." (That shift was discussed at length by my Guides in *The World Before*.)

POL told Björn that "places in the Northern Hemisphere that are today in the fiftieth degree latitude will move to what you call the twenty-fifth or twentieth degree latitude north, although naturally only one side of the Northern Hemisphere can move toward the equator, and the exact dimensions of the shift are not yet known." He said the safest survival areas will be north of the fifty-eighth degree latitude, but that there will be many other safe areas for sustaining enlightened people who will be learning to cooperate with nature and each other.

"The number of people who will survive on earth equals 10,000 multiplied by 10,000 plus one," POL declared. [I assume that means 100,000,000 plus one.] He said that they would have to be in certain areas where the disastrous poison from nuclear explosions and pollution could not harm them, and he showed Björn a vision of how cosmic beings will be able to cleanse the planet earth, breaking up the poisonous clouds by means of a gigantic electrical storm that will leave the atmosphere sweet, clean, and livable once more. "There is nothing evil created by

125

man that the Creator cannot eliminate when He wants to clean His beloved nature," he added.

The Guides foresee that nuclear weaponry, but not big bombs, will be employed in the event of World War III. Björn explains that for the detonation of a hydrogen bomb, a common uranium bomb is used as the trigger, and such elements as strontium are released, starting a continuous energy radiation that can continue for hundreds of years, killing people, animals, and plant life by destroying their organic cells. "These particles emitted by nuclear combustion can drift around the earth with winds in dust clouds for hundreds of years until their nuclear combustion ceases," he says. "These life-threatening aftereffects of the bombs can be stopped only if someone can start a chain reaction in these particles, so that they decompose in an immediate nuclear reaction. What POL means, therefore, is that the Creator can give His servants, like Power of Light, the ability to execute such a chain reaction after a nuclear war by using the power 'in' light and the universal magnetic field. It has happened before on this earth when the survivors promised the Creator to live after His codes of nature."

Björn says that POL has advised him to make drawings for a 243-foot-high model of the Great Pyramid to be built and equipped with "all the devices that you now know how to build," to receive messages and knowledge from the superconsciousness in the universal magnetic field. He said that mankind is currently capable of using only a minor part of the brain's capacity because of disturbing vibrations. "But the pyramid is a perfect antenna for the cosmic energy vibrations, and by relaxing inside the focus point of a pyramid, the possibility for man to use a major part of his brain capacity is increased and activated by the intensity of the cosmic vibrations in this focus point. If man at the same time will be affected by certain colors of light and accoustical vibrations, his brain capacity will be even more intensified. After a period of this treatment, he will be able to use the entire capacity of his brain, as it was meant to be used by the Creator. Then he will reach what we call cosmic superconsciousness, and no challenge would be too great for him. Some Walk-ins on earth today are close to this superconsciousness, but they have difficulty in reaching total brain capacity because of disturbing vibrations in their everyday surroundings."

After giving Björn the knowledge of how to build and equip such a pyramid, POL stressed that the structure will be "very necessary for the New Age people to launch the golden age on earth after the shift at the end of the century." He said that some of the superior entities who were worshipped in earlier times as deities will be returning to earth at that time, to help with the reorganization of the new society, just as Walk-ins are now returning in increasing numbers to prepare mankind for survival and a New Age free from greed and selfishness.

POL apparently considers the construction of a properly equipped pyramid essential to this preparation, because he kept stressing the point, saying, "The amplification in the pyramid can raise the information within cosmic energy from our subconscious to our conscious mind, like receiving spectacles to be able to read the divine book of universal wisdom. Since man's subconscious can receive different levels of the Creator's secrets about the process of life and matter, the receiving of this information through cosmic energy can be amplified in the pyramid partly because of the antenna form of the building itself, and partly because of the electronic and optical receiving devices tuned into certain vibrational signals. Ancient, highly developed civilizations were using similar methods in pyramids around the world."

Power of Light told Björn that there are several universes, all contained within the First Universe, which is the center of the Creator. "All the hundreds of millions of planets and stars in your own celestial sphere are moving in orbits controlled by your universal magnetic field (UMF)," he continued. "Your earth has its own magnetic field that is a part of the UMF, and in this field all the small particles that build the materia on your planet, like your body, the trees, the stones, and the sea are small atoms, and the force driving each atom in its individual pattern is your UMF. The various patterns of these nuclear movements are manifest in the diversified appearance of matter in the life forms on your planet. There is a superconsciousness in the magnetic field, and there are two kinds of vibrations: a power vibration that gives energy to the atoms to move and creates heat, which makes it possible for you to live, and there is the vibration of information of the superconsciousness of the Creator. This vibration is telling everything what it should be. It is telling water to stay as water. It's telling the plant to grow and be a

certain plant, or a fruit to be a fruit in order to feed
people and some animals, and for animals to feed on
other animals, and so on for the continuation of life
on earth. This vibration is not supposed to be disar-
ranged by man, because then he can destroy all life
on earth. This has happened before on other planets, and they are now uninhabitable for your form of
life.

"The brain works with electromagnetic waves, and
if one can enlarge the frequency area of the brain,
he can perceive more of the knowledge that exists in
the UMF and comes from the First Universe. Man
on earth is building huge radio-telescopes and transmitting messages out into the universe, hoping to
make contact with other civilizations. This procedure
is very primitive. To make contact with other civilizations in your universe you need only tune in a small
transmitter with the same frequency as that on which
a man's brain works. The weak transmitting power
from the human brain is sufficient to reach out to
other universes, and even into the First Universe if
tuned to the right vibration."

Björn says that the Egyptian pyramid builders had
knowledge of how to convert solar energy through a
crystal and concentrate the sunbeams into a more
advanced form of today's power laser. "With this device they could cut the stones easily, with the preci-
sion of one five hundredth of an inch, which is the
same laser system that I am working on for converting clean, pure energy from the sun into electric
power and hydrogen gas for propelling automobiles."

He says he has been told by POL that the missing

top of the Pyramid of Cheops was a large solar spectrum crystal, later removed by a new generation of Egyptians and split into pieces for use in the optical system at the huge lighthouse in the harbor city of Alexandria. "In its original shape and site on the Great Pyramid, the crystal was separating the visible colors from the sunbeams and the invisible power colors from the UMF," POL declared. "These separated colors were reflected into the two-chamber systems in the pyramid, where the various powers of these colors were focused in huge lenses that were moved forward and backward in the great gallery. In the revealed chamber system there are still tracks resulting from the sarcophagus being partly melted down, and the melted granite poured out over the floor from the power of the separated and focused color, the same effect that you are now building in your new mirror and lens system. The crystal that was used atop the pyramid did not come from planet Earth, but arrived as a directed meteor that landed in the northwest of Egypt and created a huge crater that is today called the Quattara Lake and which is now four hundred feet lower than the Mediterranean sea level."

At this point, overwhelmed by my own stupidity, I telephoned the Egyptian press office in Washington to see if such a thing as Quattara Lake exists. Indeed it does, was the reply. It is below sea level in the western desert of Egypt.

According to Björn and his mentors, solar energy is daily flooding the earth with twenty thousand times the energy that we are presently using. One of the vibrations is light, and the forces in light can be used individually by separating the colors in the light spectrum. "Each color contains a separate force," Björn explains, "and by mixing these forces in harmonic tunings, like tuning beautiful harmonies with certain tones at the keyboard, the desired force can be used as amplified harmonies. One color can be used for healing, both mentally and physically, by tuning the vibration for total harmony in the original body cells' vibration. Another color can be amplified in a second crystal, and at the same time be tuned together with a certain frequency from the cosmic radio signals to create a very powerful AC current by having the electrons change polarity in a magnetic field. Another color can be utilized for transforming polluted or salt water into pure drinking water by using this color's highly bacteriological cleansing effect. This color can also completely cure bacteriological and virus infections. Using a certain color together with a certain frequency from cosmic forces, persons whose physical and mental conditions are imbalanced can be transformed into complete harmony.

"The ultimate receiving antenna, and the only one for the cosmic forces is the design in any scale of the Great Pyramid. This type of building, constructed from any type of porous material and with the electronic and solar-spectrum combination can be used for focusing these forces and providing a completely new energy source for mankind on earth."

Having somewhat reluctantly become the transmitter to my readers of this scientific data, I felt that POL owed me a few down-to-earth comments about my friend Björn Örtenheim. What observations did he have on the assertions by Michael and my Guides that Björn is the Walk-in of Albert Einstein? Since I personally have no direct access to the Power of Light, I asked Björn to convey my question, and this is the response:

"The enlightened soul that entered the earth as Albert Einstein was a pure soul arriving directly from Theohim, where he had learned the cosmic science. His mission was to teach mankind more knowledge about Cosmos in order that they could understand their own planet and take care of it. But Einstein made a mistake. He overestimated the goodwill of the power elite on earth, and as a result his disclosure of nuclear power was used mainly for war-power and destruction. That's why he was so disappointed, and why he wanted to return to earth life as soon as possible, after a new training period on Theohim, to help people read the consciousness of Cosmos, the superconsciousness of the Creator."

If this is true, he spent a dozen years in that specialized training, before returning to earth life. Einstein was born in Germany in 1879, won the Nobel Prize in physics in 1921, and came to the United States in 1933, where his towering intellect made him one of the foremost citizens of the world. He died in 1955 at the age of seventy-six.

Björn Örtenheim was born in Stockholm, Sweden, to upper-class parents in 1931, and the Guides say that the transference of egos occurred in 1967, twelve years after Einstein's death, when Björn was on the verge of suicide at the age of thirty-six. Since his age at this writing is only fifty, and POL has stated that Björn will survive the shift of the earth on its axis, we can expect to hear a great deal more about this scientist-inventor in the decades ahead.

Certainly he seems to be tuned into a source that is not available to the ordinary mortal. On October 2, 1981, Björn sent me this message from Power of Light: "The leader of Egypt is in danger, and will not survive this year. Because of this, the winds of war will increase and mark the end of this particular era of mankind, before the New Age is born. Anwar Sadat is the reincarnation of Horus, and he voluntarily took this mission where he will have to sacrifice his life in trying to create understanding and peace among aggressive nations. He will have to suffer for the greed and aggressiveness of neighboring nations, and he is very aware of his dangerous mission. He was our last prophet for peace before the last great war occurs."

Four days after this message came through Björn, Anwar Sadat was assassinated.

CHAPTER VI
ANWAR SADAT

Like millions of others, I have long been a staunch admirer of Anwar Sadat, the late great president of Egypt who, in 1977, electrified the world by his historic visit to Israel. This dramatic bid for peace between warring Moslems and Jews in the volatile Middle East was unprecedented, and required incalculable bravery, since the other Arab states refused to recognize Israel's right even to exist as a nation. Thanks largely to the stunning actions of this Moslem leader, who was honored as *Time* magazine's Man of the Year in 1978 and awarded the Nobel Peace Prize together with Israeli Prime Minister Menachem Begin, the Camp David Accords came into being, and in 1979 a peace treaty between the two battle-scarred nations was signed on the south lawn of the White House.

The free world breathed a collective sigh of relief. Then came Black Tuesday, October 6, 1981, and while television cameras recorded Sadat's review of the troops on Egypt's Armed Forces Day, religious fanatics wearing the uniform of Egyptian soldiers assassinated that noble man.

Shortly before this despicable event, the Guides told me that Anwar Sadat was a Walk-in, and that the transferral of souls occurred while he was in prison. I had not been aware of his imprisonment, but was scarcely surprised, because many revolutionaries, including India's Mahatma Gandhi, had been incarcerated for their attempts to free their homelands from foreign rule.

As many of my readers are aware from my previous books, I have been irresistibly drawn to Egypt for numerous visits during the past thirty-odd years. On one of them I met Anwar Sadat briefly, when, in 1953, on the first anniversary of King Farouk's expulsion from the country, leaders of the new military government held a joint press conference for visiting newspaper reporters from all over the world. I did not, however, remark his presence, because the world spotlight was then focused on President Muhammad Naguib and his soon-to-be-successor, Gamal Abdel Nasser, whom we knew to be the real power behind the new regime.

By the time Sadat eventually succeeded to the Egyptian presidency on the death of Nasser in 1970, I had given up my nationally syndicated column on politics and world affairs, so I made no attempt to meet Sadat on his occasional visits to Washington. But after the Guides identified him to me as a Walk-in, I was looking forward to talking with him the next time that he addressed our National Press Club.

Alas, there were no further visits from this far-sighted man, and a short time after his assassination the Guides wrote: "Sadat is resting, but alert. There *are* no accidents, and he had prepared himself for the fate that he sensed awaited him. Whether he decides to reenter a human body before the shift of the earth on its axis will be a decision for him alone to make. He was a great soul in an earlier time, but we will leave that subject until later."

By now eager to check up on what the Guides had said about Sadat, I stopped in at the Egyptian press office to pick up some literature about the fallen leader, and was intrigued to read the following: "As a result of his nationalist activities, Sadat was incarcerated in a British detention camp in 1942. He succeeded in escaping from the camp and spent two years leading an underground life in Cairo as a truck driver. Surfacing after the war, he was again imprisoned by the British, finally winning his freedom in 1948."

Anwar Sadat, one of thirteen children of an Egyptian civil servant and his part-Sudanese wife, was born December 25, 1918, in a village on the Nile River Delta. The family moved to Cairo when he was twelve, and after the Abbassia Military Academy was reformed to admit lower- and middle-class applicants, young Sadat was accepted as a student. There he became friendly with Nasser, a fellow cadet. They graduated together in 1938 and were then stationed at the garrison town of Mankabad, where they and ten other young officers banded together to form a group that Sadat described as "a secret revolutionary society dedicated to the task of liberation." World War II broke out the following year, and British-controlled Egypt became a battleground, with many patriotic Egyptians, including Sadat, viewing the possibility of German victory as a God-given means of ejecting the British overlords.

After his political arrest and escape into the underground, Sadat intensified his revolutionary activities and masterminded two assassinations, one of which was bloodily successful. In his autobiography, *In Search of Identity,* the title of which seems remarkably significant for a Walk-in, Sadat frankly told of his murderous intrigues, his lies and deceits in those days before the apparent transferral of egos.

From the aliens' jail where he had previously served time, Sadat was transferred to Cairo Central Prison, a dismal hole, where he was placed in solitary confinement in Cell 54; and according to the Guides it was there that the discouraged young revolutionary finally withdrew, to make way for a Walk-in of high ideals and love of mankind. In his autobiography Sadat wrote of that strange period: "Now in the complete solitude of Cell 54, when I had no links at all with the outside world—not even newspapers or a radio—the only way in which I could break my loneliness was, paradoxically, to seek the companionship of that inner entity I call 'self.' It was not easy. A barrier seemed to stand between us. There were areas of suffering which kept that 'self' in the dark, shadows which troubled my mind and accentuated the difficulty of self-confrontation. One of these was my first marriage."

Here again was that bugaboo "marriage," which seems to affect so many Walk-outs and/or Walk-ins. Sadat, in his youth, had made a marriage of convenience with a relative, a girl from his Nile village, and it did not take the young military cadet long to discover that they had nothing in common. He was miserable in the situation, but not until many years later when he had to endure the lonely privacy of Cell 54 could he face up to the possibility of divorce. He wrote that he became "so absorbed in my soul-searching, that I was aware of the veins in my temples throbbing madly when I went to bed at night and again when I woke up in the morning. My suffering continued for a year and a half. Then one day I felt my mind had already been made up."

The night of sleep before that awakening apparently marked the withdrawal of the original personality and the advent of the Walk-in, and Sadat said that his first action was to stop his wife from paying any further visits to him in the prison. "I had finally come to know myself," he wrote. "I had finally come to know what I could, and what I could never accept, and thus began to see my route ahead clearly as never before, as well as the steps I had to take along that road."

The Guides have repeatedly stressed that when a Walk-in replaces the occupant of an adult body, he or she brings an awareness and the clear-eyed ability to solve problems that had previously seemed insurmountable. The new Walk-in is ordinarily unaware of being a different ego, because he or she inherits the memory patterns of the Walk-out, but is instantly cognizant of a remarkable alteration in attitudes, goals, and personality. Sadat said that after the morning when he awakened to the realization that a divorce was a necessity, he also discovered that there are "solutions to every problem."

"My relations with the entire universe began to be reshaped, and love became the fountainhead of all my actions and feelings," he wrote in *In Search of Identity*. "Armed with faith and perfect peace of mind, I have [thereafter] never been shaken by the turbulent events, both private and public, through which I have lived. Love never let me down."

At another point he wrote: "Love triumphed in the end. For, in fact, I cannot bring myself to hate anybody, as I am by nature committed to love. This became quite clear to me through suffering and pain, in Cell 54. . . . My love for the universe is derived from my love for God. As the Creator is my friend, I couldn't possibly be afraid of men. . . . It is He who controls their life and the entire universe. Through that feeling, which came to be an indivisible part of my very being, I was able to transcend the confines of time and place. Spatially, I did not live in a four-walled cell but in the entire universe. Time ceased to exist once my heart was taken over by the love of the Lord of all Creation. I came to feel very close to Him wherever I was. Everything came to be a source of joy and delight. All creatures became my friends. Everything in existence became an object of love, for, like it, it was made and exists through God's love for it and its love for God."

This is a superb description of the transformation that occurs when a high-minded soul replaces a previous body-occupant for the sole purpose of benefiting mankind. Sometime later, when the Nasser regime was in power and Sadat was broadcasting over the Voice of the Arabs, he wrote: "When it became clear that some people wanted to exploit the revolution by destroying all human values, I felt that I had to speak out against this and that our target should rather be to *build up mankind*. We have been created to bear the responsibility God has entrusted us with. Though different, each man should fulfill his specific vocation and shoulder his individual responsibility. To do this he should first recognize and be loyal to his real entity within, regardless of any external factors; for it is this alone which will enable him to belong and owe allegiance to that Entity which is greater, vaster, and more permanent than his individual self."

In Cell 54, he said, that belief assumed the proportions of a real faith and came to constitute an integral part of his very being. Sadat said that the ugliest feature of the new regime, after the expulsion of King Farouk, was "the mountain of hate which accumulated in the course of the attempt to build a power-based community." And significantly he wrote of himself: "Inside Cell 54 as my material needs grew increasingly less, the ties which had bound me to the material world began to be severed, one after another. My soul, having jettisoned its earthly freight, was freed and so took off like a bird soaring into space, into the furthest regions of existence, into infinity.

"This is why I regard my last eight months in prison as the happiest period in my life. It was then that I was initiated into that new world of self-abnegation which enabled my soul to merge into all other beings, to expand and establish communion with the Lord of all Being. ... My narrow self ceased to exist and the only recognizable entity was the totality of existence, which aspired to a higher, transcendental reality. ... My paramount object was to make people happy. I identified with people's joys. Such despicable emotions as hate and vengeance were banished. To love no longer meant to possess, but rather to let yourself be absorbed into another person's soul, to give and lose yourself in another person's being."

Such lyricism is common to some who call themselves born-again Christians. They joyfully describe what happened to them after they "took Jesus Christ into my life," or after they "gave myself to Jesus Christ."

The problem here is that Anwar Sadat was not a Christian. He was a devout Moslem, and as such certainly did not accept Jesus as the only son of God. The Guides say that many, although by no means all, of those who call themselves born-again Christians are in fact Walk-ins, but having never heard of the process by which a high-minded soul comes directly from the spirit plane to exchange places with a discouraged, unhappy, dying or troubled soul, they are unaware of the transition.

Anwar Sadat, after thirty-one months in jail, gained his freedom. He promptly obtained a divorce, and in 1949 married the beautiful Jihan, whom he met following his release from imprisonment. The rest is history, and it is not an exaggeration to say that the "new" Anwar Sadat, who helped to mastermind the bloodless coup that overthrew King Farouk and to set up a new elective form of government, came to be admired as one of the greatest leaders of modern times.

I asked the Guides for further comment on Sadat, and they wrote: "Sadat is now watching from this side [the spirit plane] and is pleased with the progress that his successor is making in his beloved Egypt. Before he became Anwar Sadat through the Walk-in process he had been an Egyptian of great renown. He loved every inch of that barren country, especially along the Nile, where life flowed through a desert land. When he became aware of the utter discouragement of the man in prison, and of his desire to leave that body and that stinking prison, he gladly stepped in, bringing with him awareness and a desire for peace. The transferral occurred in the darkest hour of that solitary prison confinement, and his Walk-out predecessor is here now, saying, 'If I had devoted myself to love instead of hatred, and had sought peaceful ways to overthrow the British in my country, it would not have become necessary for me to leave. But I was deeply discouraged, hopeless, and unwilling to face a longer time in incarceration. I willingly stepped out so that a greater soul might use that body to help my homeland. Praise Allah!' The one the world now remembers as Sadat is equally devoted to his homeland, but eager to bring peace to the entire Middle East. He has no resentments against those who assassinated him. He will soon decide whether again to become a Walk-in, to speed the process of a peaceful solution for the problems of the Jewish and Moslem states. He wishes now to reemphasize the importance of integrity and love."

It is possible, therefore, that we who are living today may not have seen the last of Anwar Sadat, although if he comes again as a Walk-in he will be bearing another's name and countenance.

CHAPTER VII
CAROL KIMMEL

Like a mother who retains a unique sentiment for her firstborn, no matter how many other children subsequently join the family circle, I feel a special attachment to Carol Kimmel of Solana Beach, California, because she was the first Walk-in to contact me after reading *Strangers Among Us*.

The print must scarcely have been dry on the book's pages when her letter came, fervently thanking me for writing the book that had helped her to understand the revolutionary changes in her life. Although several letters arrived about the same time from other readers who believed themselves to be Walk-ins, hers was the only one that earned from the

Guides their seal of endorsement: "Carol Kimmel is indeed a Walk-in."

Carol's letter, written in early September 1979, confided: "I have had an unusual fifteen months, starting after a long period of time during which I begged all the forces in my power to let me out of a life situation that I could no longer face. I had a loving husband, two children, and a stressful period of court reporting school, and I was botching the whole thing. The guilt of failure was so awful that I couldn't face my family or friends any longer, and although I never considered suicide, I desperately wanted *out.*

"Then two incidents occurred which changed my life. I had begun meditating for hours at a time, both day and night. I definitely felt presences around me, gentle puffs of air on my lips and cheeks, clicks and pops in the immediate vicinity of my meditation, and one night my meditation area was lit with a beautiful glow. I could almost see divine figures moving about in the room, looking carefully at the furnishings and the articles with which I had surrounded myself, as if they were taking a character reading of me. Simultaneously I felt very distinctly that my urgent prayers for release would be answered.

"Then one evening, while sitting passively with my back against the couch, I suddenly felt as if the life-force had whooshed out of my body through the top of my head, collapsing me as though I were a puppet and the strings had been cut, first my feet and then all the way to the top of my body, and I slid to the side. I became totally aware of my cellular structure glowing softly and thought, This must be death. Then I lost consciousness."

Carol does not know how long the coma lasted, but she reports: "The following weeks found me ecstatic, amazed at the newness of the world, and enchanted with my two little children who suddenly became my best friends. My husband was upset when I couldn't control the energies pouring through me—I seemed for a time to be living two lives at the same time—and after a particularly distressing episode I was taken to the local mental health clinic, where I was put on a mood stabilizing drug. Then a horrible period of depression followed, until I finally refused to take the drug that was being administered through a mistaken diagnosis."

Carol's letter said that since then her life had changed completely. She immediately dropped out of the court reporting school because that way of earning money no longer appealed to her, and she had no interest in "keeping up with the Joneses" by having extra money for new cars and possessions.

"I began stopping by the local day-care center that my daughter was attending while I had been in school, and playing a few chords on my guitar," she continued. "Now I am there daily, teaching music and movement to children and finding my life and associations very valuable and dear. It is a New Age school devoted to nurturing the children, and they have nurtured me as well. The world looks new and beautiful to me."

With Carol's permission, I passed along her interesting letter to Laura, the young woman who first introduced me to the subject of Walk-ins, and whose story I recounted in *Strangers Among Us*. Thus began a three-way correspondence between Carol, Laura, and myself, and the two attractive young Walk-ins wrote frequently to each other, sending carbons of their letters to me.

Laura's understanding and suggestions were extremely valuable to Carol, who, after receiving her first letter from Laura, wrote back: "It was the confirmation I needed for my final acceptance of the truth that I am a Walk-in. I do believe it now. I used to be able to recapture feelings, moods, and emotions with music, always managing somehow to put myself back into the picture and relive the scene. Now I not only cannot do that with the memories I have of *before* the transition, but I can't seem to recapture things in that way *after* the transition. It is as though I have changed my orientation somehow, that I no longer perceive myself as a jigsaw puzzle personality, but rather as an entity living in an eternal 'present' state. Mental images now have a 'hereness' and a 'nowness' about them."

Making reference to the excruciating head pains that Laura experienced just before her own transferral of egos a year previously, Carol wrote: "My own pain seemed to be a spiritual rather than a physical one. As long as I live I will never forget those moments when I found myself absolutely alone inside my skull, when my voice echoed in my head, and my body seemed to have split in dead center, one half working independently of the other half. I have never felt so lost, so despairing, because I had made such a terrible error that for eternity I was to be locked in an endless grip with the forces of light and darkness struggling within. Really, it was a scene worthy of *Star Trek.*"

Fortunately for her peace of mind, Carol realized that she was a different soul, and not a split personality, but she kept that knowledge from family and friends for fear they would not understand. Her husband had asked her about the "Dear Laura" and "Dear Ruth" letters he had noticed in her typewriter, but she had "put him off."

"He accepted being shut out, because my predecessor had hidden herself away from him for many years, and this family was hanging together by his loyal determination alone," she wrote ruefully. Then she decided to tell Joel, and made careful preparations. "I showed him the book jacket for *Strangers Among Us,* and he read Ruth's rather impressive credentials. Then I asked him to read the book through Chapter Six, and I would show him the letters, and we would talk about my Big Secret at last. I had expected any number of reactions—disbelief, humor, even anger—and was ready to be as dispassionate and open as I could be. He read the book and the letters, looked at me calmly, and said, 'I believe you.' Well, I was bugged. I had been wrestling with this since September, and he believed me! I exclaimed that it sounded crazy, but he replied, 'Don't make it difficult. I don't know why I believe you, but I do.' And in the ensuing conversation it became quite clear that he wasn't just humoring me. Maybe there have been more changes in me, outwardly at least, than I had perceived. Maybe at some level of consciousness he understood a little bit of what was happening. He is a level-headed, feet-on-the-ground fellow, a talented industrial filmmaker highly respected in his field, but he does have a mystical side. He writes beautiful songs and occasional screenplays. I can see that I'm going to have to get to know him all over again."

A short time later Carol again wrote about her husband, who is media director for a large corporation. Expressing her admiration for his character, she said, "My predecessor in this body had thought of him very differently. I can see depths within him that had not been seen before. It is interesting to start to react to him in the 'old' way, and then to realize that these are not *my* reactions at all, but *hers,* and I have to stop and think things through all over again. Her memories still determine my actions sometimes, but she and I are becoming farther and farther apart. It's difficult to recapture her motives. Sometimes I think there must be a trick to tapping into the memory bank [of the Walk-out], because so much of that which deals with the emotional side of the nature seems not to be recorded. The factual memory is clear and detailed, but the emotional memory is not always there. This is hard to describe!"

In preparing this book, I asked Carol to tell me something of her early life, and she said that she was born in San Diego in 1942, the daughter of "a dashing air force officer and a pretty mother" who worked in an office during World War II while Carol's father was flying dangerous missions over France and Germany. At that time she and her mother lived with her grandparents, who petted and indulged her, but with her father's return they moved to their own apartment and she became, in her words, "an out-of-control, undisciplined brat" who earned frequent punishments from her father and learned fear of men. She scored high on I.Q. tests but made poor grades, because of her "laziness and lack of interest."

What she lacked in self-discipline she made up for in appearance. A stunningly beautiful girl who resembled Grace Kelly, at the age of eighteen she left home to take a small apartment with another girl and a low-paying sales job, while attending night school at the city college. Later, after a failed marriage that lasted less than a year, she traveled for a time with German friends, before meeting Joel and starting a new life with him in Solana Beach. This second marriage lasted fourteen years and produced two children to whom Carol is devoted, but since becoming a Walk-in the marriage has been dissolved.

This is by no means an isolated occurrence when a different soul enters the body of one who had created his or her own entangling alliances. Carol says that she felt deep respect for Joel, but could not "fall in love" with him, and out of a sense of fairness felt that she should release him to continue with the type of society that he and the former Carol had enjoyed.

The relationship was obviously not working too smoothly before the transition, as the original Carol had so desperately wanted "out" of life, but the "new" Carol's interests are totally changed. "I accept the metaphysical as I accept gravity," she explains. "It is natural. It is reasonable. I am not swept away by it, as I am not swept away by photosynthesis. It is marvelous, but so is all of life, and no aspect of life demands my total attention to the exclusion of all else. This is quite different than the thinking of my predecessor in this body."

Having grown in her dimensions, Carol now holds security clearance and a challenging job with a scientific company, where she is surrounded by technical scientists who are exploring the mysteries of our universe for practical ends. She has also taken up skiing and sailing, and is experiencing other new challenges, but she says of the marriage failure:

"I have regrets. Tonight as I tucked my daughter into bed she asked if I could be home tomorrow, so that she could walk home from school. I could not. I have to be at the office five days a week, and I cannot indulge her and myself by taking the time off to fulfill the role that was filled when she lived in an intact family. But perhaps in the future, when the institutions and traditions give way to the massive changes that are coming her way, she will not be locked into set ways of life-style, and she will be able to deal with newness, change, and nontraditional ways of being, even though her ideal and mine at present is to have Mommy at home when she comes from school. I must believe this, or my regret for the marriage not working out would be too great. Her father is now remarried, and I'm sure much more contented."

Carol has obviously been doing a lot of soul-searching in her new role as a Walk-in, and the Guides have several times commented that she has not yet "found her place" in the scheme of things, although she is certainly trying. One of their comments was: "She entered that body in order to assist others and to take over from a badly frightened girl whose problems seemed insurmountable because of her mental state. Carol entered to straighten out her affairs, before pressing onward to help prepare mankind for the difficult years ahead, although she has not yet found the key to that performance."

The Guides have often stressed that when exchanging places with a Walk-out, the Walk-in must pledge to solve the problems of the predecessor before moving on to his or her own projects in serving humanity. It would seem, therefore, that Carol is presently working her way through that initial step.

While completing this chapter, I asked again about this beautiful woman, and the Guides wrote: "Carol Kimmel will soon find herself as she meets and talks with other Walk-ins who will seek her out after the book is published. She will become a gentle leader of the New Age people, and will find within herself great depths of power and intuition." Carol had experienced some reluctance to make her identity known, but the Guides added reassuringly: "Tell her not to worry, as she will not be embarrassed by her appearance in the book, but rather will find herself admired and sought after as a speaker and counselor."

It is true that Carol has felt lonely and isolated since becoming a Walk-in, because unlike many of them she does not know other Walk-ins in her area with whom she can talk and share experiences and goals. Nor do I know others in the San Diego area, although I am sure that there are dozens of them.

Walk-ins have a way of finding one another after a time, but Carol is a relatively new one, and if this book can do no more than assist in bringing isolated Walk-ins together to merge their talents and their purposes, it will not have been published in vain. Time is of the essence for all of us.

CHAPTER VIII
HARRY COLLINS

Dr. Elisabeth Kubler-Ross and I were to be the speakers at a seminar aboard the M.S. *World Renaissance,* during a Caribbean cruise in early December 1981. I was looking forward to meeting the Swiss psychiatrist whose pioneering work with the terminally ill was attracting international attention, for although I had not read her books in the field of death and dying, I had heard enough about her to consider that she might be a Walk-in, because of her dedication to helping others. In fact, it was principally with that idea in mind that I accepted the invitation of Giovanna Holbrook, sponsor of the workshop, to be a speaker at such a busy time.

The ship sailed Saturday night from San Juan, and on Sunday I was introduced to Dr. Kubler-Ross, whose first words to me were, "You were the reason I came on this cruise. I wanted to meet you."

This heightened my expectation that there was a purpose behind our encounter, and as we came to know each other better, I asked if she felt that she was a Walk-in. "I don't know," she replied, "but I would like to know. Let's ask our Guides, and see what they say." I do not know what answer she may have received from her own counselors, but the next morning I put the question to my Guides, and to my disappointment they replied in the negative, saying that although Dr. Ross was not a Walk-in, she was a highly developed soul who was performing an important mission for the benefit of humanity.

That day I delivered my first lecture to the assembled group on shipboard, while we anchored off Barbados, and following a discussion of Walk-ins I asked if anyone in the audience felt that he or she might be one. Unlike some such gatherings where several hands are raised, no one responded to the challenge; but that evening a young woman approached me and suggested that I talk to a man known to her only as Harry, who had apparently undergone a strange experience. I gladly made a date for the following day, and despite some initial reluctance to talk about himself, he gradually told me such fascinating details about his life-and-death experience that I later consulted the Guides, who readily declared: "Yes, Harry Collins* is definitely a

*A pseudonym.

Walk-in and will be heard from in more ways than one, as he finds his niche and begins working with others for improving the lot of mankind in these decades ahead."

G. Harry Collins was one of the few attending the seminar who had not read *Strangers Among Us* or heard of Walk-ins. He had joined the cruise because of his developing interest in work with the terminally ill and to try to sort out and analyze the strange occurrences that seemed to be drastically changing his life. Although he lives in Maryland, not too far from my home in Washington, D.C., it is unlikely that our paths would have crossed except for the seeming "coincidence" of our both wishing to meet and hear Elisabeth Kubler-Ross.

In interviews aboard ship, and later at my residence in Washington, I learned many details about the tall, light-blue-eyed, fifty-nine-year-old man whose dark hair is streaked with gray.

His story may be said to have begun in 1974 when, during a routine physical examination at Anne Arundel General Hospital in Maryland, microscopic traces of blood showed up in a urine test. One year later his urine was "loaded with it," and he was told to check back yearly for reexamination.

"On the basis of those instructions, which didn't make it sound very serious," he says, "I was married that December. Six months later, my kidneys suddenly went dead. They took a biopsy, and after that I had to drive to Baltimore General Hospital three days a week, spending four hours each time on a dialysis machine. Eventually they opened up a dialysis center in our community, and my treatments were stepped up to five hours a day, but even this couldn't keep step with the accumulating uremic poisoning in my system."

After his weight plummeted from 204 to 134 pounds, he was transferred to Georgetown Hospital in Washington, D.C., where he was on dialysis five days a week for five hours a day, and was also receiving blood transfusions. Every known test, from electrolyte imbalance to CAT scans, was made on Collins, but no cause could be found for his alarming condition. All that the medical team could determine was that his kidneys were dead, and that in only one of a hundred thousand cases did dialysis fail to rid the body of uremic poisoning. After Collins' parathyroids were removed, to no avail, the head physician finally wrote on his case summary: "Unfortunately we are at the end of our diagnostics."

In early June 1979 Harry was pronounced a terminal case, and told that with daily continuation on a dialysis machine he would probably live until Christmas. Without the treatment he might have ten days. I have seen his medical reports, and the final one on which his doctor at Georgetown Hospital wrote: "Patient wants to stop dialysis. Feels quality of life is not acceptable."

Collins went home to die. He made a will, planned his funeral arrangements, said good-bye to his family, and prepared himself for the buildup of uremic poisoning that would end his life. It was better to go then, he decided, than to put his family through the traumatic ordeal of a deathwatch and funeral during the Christmas season.

The end was near when, at 2:20 A.M. on June 20,

he received a long-distance call from Georgetown Hospital to come at once. A twenty-year-old man killed in a motorcycle accident had previously signed a donor card, and his kidneys matched Collins' in the minimum twenty-six ways. It seemed like a miracle, as Harry's five adult children by a previous marriage had already been tested as possible donors, but none of their kidneys sufficiently matched their father's to risk a transplant.

Collins recalls getting into his car for the race against time to Georgetown Hospital forty miles away. He vaguely remembers his car hitting the curb in the hospital's parking lot, and then his being put on dialysis for a final clearing before the operation, but nothing else. He has no conscious memory of the next five days. On the sixth night he had a hallucination in which he felt like a fish bumping into the sides of a goldfish bowl that was proving an insurmountable barrier between him and the rest of the world. On the seventh night, in another nightmare, he was struggling with the parents of the deceased donor who kept demanding that the kidney be returned, saying, "Our son gave you his kidney so that your life could be spared, but you're not a whole person. You're not making it, and we want it back."

"My body kept insisting that the kidney was mine," Collins says, "and the struggle to keep it was sheer torture. The eighth night was even worse. Something was trying to stop my mind from joining my body, and I was hysterically sobbing. It was like a hurricane raging inside of me, while I was conscious of a nurse at my bedside who kept saying, 'Just hold my hand. Hold on. We'll pray together.' Then, as when a tropical storm has played itself out and the sun comes through, with birds singing and the air tranquil, I awakened the next morning 'together' again. I then learned that the nurse had sat with me for fourteen hours, refusing to leave when her tour of duty was over."

Collins says that for the previous three years he had been so despondent that he had scarcely spoken. Now he never stopped. "I must have sounded like a babbling idiot," he says with a rueful grin. "I couldn't shut up. I wouldn't let anyone else finish a sentence, because I knew what all of them were going to say and would finish it for them. When doctors were preparing to take my blood pressure, or that of other patients, I would tell them exactly what the reading was going to show, and it always did. I knew what was going on in the rooms around me. Hospital psychiatrists would call out two numbers of four digits each (like 2783 x 7621) and I could mentally multiply them faster than the calculators could check my correct answers. I could call the fourteenth card, or whatever, in an unopened deck. It was weird!"

He discovered to his discomfort that he could also read people's minds at a distance, and when in a somnolent state would sometimes write down what he seemed to be hearing, only to discover that the person in question had actually spoken those words to someone else at that time. "But I don't do that anymore," he avers. "I've made myself stop interfering with other people's privacy."

His wife, Jane, had been a tower of strength throughout his long ordeal, but not long after his return to their house she asked for a legal separation.

"It was a shock," Harry muses. "But with all that she'd been through for me, she could have had anything she wanted, even the separation, although she wouldn't say why she wanted it. I couldn't argue with her, so I called in the family lawyer who had been best man at our wedding." The attorney was equally puzzled, believing that Jane still loved Harry, but she refused to state her reasons, and after signing the legal separation he moved to his club. There he began to make new discoveries about himself.

"It's quite a change, but suddenly nothing could upset me," he says simply. "I'm never angry. No one's opinion bothers me, because even if it's diametrically opposed to my own, he or she has a right to it. I like foods that used to turn me off. Money has no interest for me personally, but before I used to think a lot about it. I was making better than a hundred thousand a year in my floor-covering business, before selling it, but I let it all go."

Collins says that at the time of their legal separation he turned over everything that he had, including the house and investments, to his wife, keeping for himself only $259 in his checking account, and his disability Social Security pension. Sometime later he discovered that he had inadvertently failed to sign over to his wife his share of eleven acres that he owned with a friend. Using knowledge that he did not know he possessed, he quickly devised plans for an industrial park to be located there, and took them to one of the top building engineers in Maryland, who looked them over and calculated that there would be 67,000 feet of rentable space. Collins, with absolutely no engineering experience, insisted that the plan would provide 113,450 square feet, plus space for a fountain and courtyard, and he says he was proved right.

The engineer made a careful study and estimated that it would cost $975,000 to move the dirt, but Collins, pointing out a different system of construction, said there would be no dirt to move. And there wasn't.

"In two days on the telephone I raised two million dollars for financing," he recalls, "and when we needed more, I presented a new system of financing that had never before been tried. Our lawyer laboriously wrote it out in fifteen typed pages, but still couldn't solve the problem. Then, while he swore at me good-naturedly, I dashed it off in three sentences at his desk, and it was approved by twenty-three insurance companies.

"Top engineers advised me to forget about applying for city water for the project, since the eleven-acre plot is outside the city limits. I therefore went before the city council, intending to ask for an extension of time, but within minutes they had unanimously voted to approve the water request, the first time in five years that they'd granted such a supply for use outside of town."

Collins stressed that he is not boasting about these accomplishments. His attitude is rather that of a person who marvels at how easily things now fall into place, as if there were unseen guidance. Strangers have come up to him and asked, "Are you a Master?" A woman sat down beside him in an airplane and suddenly remarked, "I think I have healing powers in my hands, but how can I convince my daughter?" He had never seen her before. Others come to him with their problems. The head of a department at a large university hospital has repeatedly asked him to reorganize its facilities.

Meanwhile, he is doing much needed work as a volunteer aide to the terminally ill. I am aware of some of his cases, and of his seeming ability to find the right words to say to these dying patients and their loved ones. Surely there was little in the background of the busy executive before the kidney transplant that could account for such an altered personality, unless a new soul had indeed entered his body.

Eager to grasp a more complete understanding of this intriguing man, I talked with his ex-wife, Jane. I asked if she noticed any personality or psychological alteration in her husband following his near-brush with death, and she replied with assurance, "Yes, very much so! When he finally awakened a week or so following the kidney transplant, he could foresee things that were going to happen. He had never before shown any signs of extrasensory perception, but now he seemed able to read people's minds. Although he had been reasonably good at figures before, he could certainly not do the mental multiplications in four figures that he was doing afterward. He knew nothing about engineering, but suddenly he seemed to know all about it. Better than the trained engineers."

She said that when she took him home from the hospital it was as though she were living with a stranger. Of that difficult period, she recalls, "I had felt during his recuperation in the hospital that he was a different person. Not the same one I had known before. When we came home it became even more apparent. He would have strange outbursts. He showed no appreciation for what his children and I had been through with him during the four years of his desperate illness. He dropped his friends. I began to feel that every time he looked at me he was distastefully remembering the dialysis machine. There was no love left. I finally decided that the only salvation would be a legal separation, and he moved to his club. Then he totally changed. He resumed some of the earlier friendships and made new friends among the executives, lawyers, and other professional men who belong to the club. His old hostilities were gone, along with the anger and self-interest."

Knowing that Jane had not read *Strangers Among Us* and was previously unfamiliar with the term Walk-in, I asked, "Do you feel that a different soul now occupies his body?"

Without hesitation, she replied, "I thought so in the hospital, although I'd never heard of such a thing. Now I'm sure of it. He is totally unlike the G. Harry Collins I used to know."

The breakup of their marriage is not, of course, unusual. In most of the cases that I have personally encountered, such a rift has occurred either just before or just after a Walk-in takes the place of the Walk-out. Sometimes an unhappy marriage is the immediate "cause" of a walk out, and sometimes the "effect." The latter is understandable, since a new person with different emotional and personality attributes has replaced the original occupant of the body, and is no longer in harmony with the existing husband or wife.

And what does Collins plan to do with the money that he expects to receive as his share of the industrial park project? Unhesitatingly he replied, "I plan to build an in-place facility where terminal patients who have no one to look after them at home can go for loving care and counseling by volunteers, so that when their time comes they can die with dignity. I've already drawn the plans for the center. It will have forty rooms, a vegetable garden, and an area for cattle and pigs, which friends have agreed to donate."

Aware of his limited income, I asked if he would not keep some of it for himself, and he replied, "No, I learned during my own terminal illness how little you can take with you. God doesn't give you what you want, He gives you what you need, and I don't need much. You can't believe how totally happy I am! I have too much energy and love. I'm attracting people like a dog does fleas. The barber takes me into his confidence. I get constant calls for help, and I love it. Cats and dogs run to me for petting. I must be the happiest man alive. When I really need something, it seems to fall into my lap. The other day my insurance agent died, and the man who took over his clients called to tell me that I had six thousand dollars of accumulated dividends. I didn't even know the policy paid dividends."

He says doctors have suggested that he write a layman's book on nephrology, which a physician can hand to patients who are faced with the necessity of undergoing dialysis or a transplant. He is also working on a theory to make the time that one spends on a dialysis machine productive and cheerful, doing away with those hate-filled hours of resentment.

After several talks with Collins, it seemed indicative to me that a different soul had taken over his body at some point following the kidney transplant. I asked the Guides if they could pinpoint the transferral more precisely, and they said that it occurred during the two-hour coma after his nightmares ceased. He then awakened refreshed and "together again."

In other words, when it became apparent in the spirit plane that the original occupant of the body could not pull through despite the transplant, the present Harry Collins exchanged places with the dying man and recharged the vital life signs. The Guides say of this transition: "The original occupant withdrew during the coma, and the present one has since revitalized the body and is interested in helping others. In an earlier life he was a chemist who worked to prolong life. He will revolutionize the treatment of the elderly during this particular lifetime, as he is developing ideas brought over from spirit that will induce longevity, as well as bringing comfort to those who are terminally ill."

At a later date I asked the Guides if they could tell me anything about the previous occupant of Collins' body, and they wrote: "He is here now, and thrilled beyond belief that such a soul would have taken over that wasted body, rejuvenated it, and begun such an important work. He sends his love to Harry, and says, 'Carry on, old man. I'm pulling for you.'"

Last of all I spoke with Dr. Marcia Chambers, the clinical psychologist in Georgetown University Hospital's psychiatry department who has frequently examined Collins since his kidney transplant. She is familiar with the alterations in his character and abilities, and when I explained to her the concept of Walk-ins, she declared: "I can't rule it out! I know of no logical medical explanation at the present time for these cases where a complete metamorphosis occurs after a near-death experience. The concept is very interesting. It's a brand new world that my patient has entered, and I think it's good for him to know that there are others who have undergone similar experiences. It seems to have settled him. It was probably not just a 'coincidence' that he met and talked with you on the cruise."

CHAPTER IX
CAROL PARRISH

One of the most tantalizing assertions made by the Guides in *Strangers Among Us* was that Walk-ins would shortly be willing to reveal their true identities. They said that secrecy would no longer be necessary, since Walk-ins were now entering adult bodies at such an increased tempo that people would soon accept their presence with pleasure, realizing that they are enlightened souls who have returned in this rather unorthodox fashion solely to aid mankind during the troublesome decades ahead. Since then I seem to meet them or hear about them wherever I go.

One such encounter, as previously noted, oc-

curred on a Caribbean cruise ship when I unexpectedly met Harry Collins, who had not heard of Walk-
ins but was acutely aware that something momentous
had happened to him during a near-death experience. Another case was also brought to my attention
on that cruise, when, at the start of my lecture, I
asked if anyone in the audience knew a Walk-in. Responding, an attractive titian-haired woman said she
believed that a prominent minister of her acquain-
tance is one, and I made a date to speak with her
afterward.

Rusty Petters and her husband, Jim, who have a
paramedical business in Cocoa, Florida, said that
they had joined the cruise because of their long-time
interest in the psychic field, and when I promised
not to divulge the name of the minister without her
own permission, they readily mentioned their good
friend Carol Parrish. The name was immediately familiar to me, because although I had not met the
Reverend Carol Parrish of Sarasota, Florida, I recognized her as a well-known metaphysical minister who
is much sought after as a lecturer at seminars in the
psychic field. In fact, she had once telephoned me to
ask that I address a retreat in Florida, but unfortunately I was unable to do so at that time.

On my return home from the cruise, I asked the
Guides about Carol Parrish and was told that she is
indeed a Walk-in. I thereupon contacted Rusty with
this confirming news, and after she had spoken with
Carol she relayed the information to me that I could
telephone her directly.

Carol, a vivacious brunette in her late forties, had
fortunately read *Strangers Among Us,* and seemed not

in the least surprised to learn that the Guides had identified her as a Walk-in. "I think I can handle that," she said, with a smile in her voice. "In fact, I've been wondering if this were so ever since I read your last book. It would logically explain the remarkable transformation of my personality and goals after a near-death experience in 1958."

She said that at the age of twenty-three she was in labor with her sixth child, and to ease her pains the attending physician gave her a shot of sodium pentothal, an ordinarily safe drug to which she had a violent allergic reaction.

"My lungs collapsed," she recalled, "and I was suddenly floating near the ceiling, unaware of who I was or what was happening. Then I looked down at the hospital bed and saw a silver cord protruding from the top of a woman's head, to which I was attached. I felt like a balloon, bobbing up and down, and just as I realized that the woman on the bed was 'me,' I saw her give birth. I could see the baby plainly, and that it was a girl.

"Then there was a rushing feeling, and I soared out into space, aware of the stars, and of an inner peace that I had never before experienced. I could sense a magnificent Presence, who comforted me and made me aware that there was no difference between what we call life and death. It was all part of a divine pattern. This powerful Presence had no discernible form, but seemed to be the embodiment of liquid love. I don't know how else to describe it. Love energy permeated my being. I could feel it moving within me, and I received waves of spiritual insight. I understood life and death, and all fear vanished. A new serenity enfolded me, and the awareness that absorbed my being can only be called bliss. Time lost all meaning. I was bathed in love and light. Then I lost consciousness."

Finally she began to awaken, and as she tried to tell her doctor and a Catholic priest about her soul-shaking experience, they both tut-tutted her, and called it hallucination. "But from then on, my life changed dramatically," Carol says. "I was no longer the person I had been."

Reminiscing about her earlier life, she said that she was regarded by her mother and stepfather as a "sensitive, or peculiar, child," and that she "knew psychically when they were trying to deceive me." At the age of sixteen, just out of high school, she married and had one pregnancy after another, year after year. "My husband and I had a lot of marital problems," she continued. "He was a fireman, and a loner. With all of those children I was swamped, overwhelmed, physically and emotionally exhausted. It was an impossible task, and I received no assistance from him. I felt absolutely hopeless. Life seemed one long dark tunnel, and I would gladly have left it, except what would then happen to the children? We were living in Dunedin, Florida, and were extremely poor. I was passive in my approach to life. My path was to endure.

"After my near-death experience I suddenly became outgoing and achieving. I went back to school to study bookkeeping, took a job, and before long became accounts control manager for the local bank. My aggressive new approach to life was very threatening for my husband. He felt that he had lost control. He was unwilling to have his wife work, although I *had* to work to help support the children. Then I joined a financial advisory service as counselor, and began earning such an excellent income that it gave my husband his freedom to leave us."

Freed at last from her marital bonds, which had been forged by her predecessor in that body, Carol attended a lecture at the Temple of the Living God in St. Petersburg, and was startled when an elderly woman named Ann Manser walked over to her and said, "I've been waiting for you." At that time Carol was still a practicing Catholic, and felt uncomfortable about the strange approach, but soon afterward she enrolled in a series of self-development classes offered by Manser and other Spiritualist ministers, and following several years of study was ordained in 1971 as a metaphysical minister.

Since then she has devoted full time to her ministry, preaching, training other teachers; and six years ago founded the Villa Serena, a small spiritual community in Sarasota, Florida. In 1974 Carol served on the President's Council on the Status of Women in America, and in 1980 was keynote speaker at the International Women's Peace Conference in Toronto, before flying on to India to lecture before the United Nations Federation and to talk with Prime Minister Indira Gandhi. She is now a member of the board of trustees for the National Council of Community Churches, and has been "moving more into the mainstream of New Age Christianity, to bridge the gap between the esoteric and dogmatic beliefs, and encourage ecumenical efforts."

Since the transferral of egos occurred, countless

people have commented on Carol's excessive energy and drive, and the Guides have said that Walk-ins bring in a supercharged energy. Carol says of the change: "I am described as intense. There is a single-mindedness of purpose in my life that I think being a Walk-in may explain. My feelings of 'mission' and 'message' rule my life. I feel that an enlightened one should be able to see the seriousness of our times and realize how fortunate are those who are embodied at this time. I feel a sense of urgency and responsibility. My children have resented my public work for the most part, and the attention attracted to us has been very hard on and for them."

It is true that Carol seems to devote less time to her now-grown children than the average mother, but if the Walk-in concept is correct they are actually the offspring of the previous Carol, who "died" in childbirth. In fact, an astrologer who worked on Carol's horoscope can find "absolutely no karmic ties" between Carol and any of her children, which is extremely unusual in a normal family relationship.

Carol, in commenting on this situation, wrote to me: "The ties of parent and children continue through the personalities to be important ones. Obligations are honored by the Walk-in, but the intense energy of the life must be directed to the spiritual reason for coming into a body. All souls have daily learning experiences that create growth, although it is usually veiled from view. The Walk-in has a very thin veil over the spiritual work. In other words, the personality is less and less important and the mission or message is paramount. The love ties have to alter to be spiritual ties, to keep them charged. This way an even deeper tie can be created. My personal concern is that the children and my parents feel deeply loved, not further alienated by a new way of looking at our personal relationship."

The Guides have repeatedly stressed that a Walk-in must agree to "finish the projects of his or her predecessor" before embarking on a new program to aid mankind in general, and Carol Parrish is a living example of that maxim. She became a Walk-in during the birth of her sixth child, and despite the suddenly altered personality, with its new goals and purposes, she continued to bear children for the man she had ceased to love. She explains:

"I think it is important to understand that when a Walk-in enters, there remains the body, and something of the emotional and mental nature of the previous personality. These become the tools for the new soul to use. Ties are still honored and karmic commitments are assumed for satisfactory completion. Never was this more clear to me than when, after the birth of my youngest son, I was warned by the doctor never to have another child. I broke down in tears, telling him, 'I have one more child, a girl, I must bear.' I knew I had that to do. Two and a half years later she was born, and I had completed the obligation begun by the previous soul."

In the years since then Carol says that she has had many visions, and that in 1981 she received a strong psychic message to found a new community in Oklahoma. Move to Oklahoma? Leave the comfortable and productive life she was enjoying in Sarasota? The idea sounded nonsensical, yet how to ignore it? Carol says of that traumatic dilemma: "I can't say to the public and my students, 'Follow your inner guidance,' and then ignore my own. I have to follow it, or I can't maintain my own integrity. When I was told 'Oklahoma,' my heart fell. Oklahoma in my mind was like an outpost of civilization. It certainly held no attraction for me. I went strictly from a sense of obedience, and I'm not normally a particularly obedient person."

Carol and her present husband, Charles Harra, a university business manager, dutifully flew to Oklahoma, and following intuitive guidance selected three hundred acres in a rather isolated area at the end of a road ten miles from Tahlequah, which in turn is sixty-five miles southeast of Tulsa. They called their new community Sparrow Hawk Village, for the name of the mountain into which it nestles, and the focus of the community will be the Light of Christ Community Church, of which Carol is the pastor, at the top of the mountain. Five families have already taken up residence there, and more are planning to move to Sparrow Hawk Village soon, from Florida and other areas. Part of the heavily wooded land already has been cleared for orchards, gardens, crops, and ponds that will be shared by the residents. Row houses will be clustered on lanes that follow hillside contours, and will be earth-sheltered to conserve energy and natural resources.

"Our community is not to be confused with a commune," Carol emphasizes. "Its citizens will own their individual cluster-homes and have an undivided interest in the common area. Some clusters will be on the mountaintop near the church, and others will be situated at the base of the mountain. Everything says that community is the way in the New Age. We do not want a retirement village. We don't want to segregate ourselves from the cycles of life. As a mother I well remember how hard it was to meet the physical and emotional needs of my family, after having worked all day to make a living. How I wished for aunts, uncles, and grandparents who loved the children and could encourage me! We can do that for each other. Today in many areas there are no open fields, swimming holes, or orchards, and parents fear to have their children out of sight for very long. Children grow up warned of the danger humanity creates. We believe that the active step of creating a place of beauty and high principles is a kind of service that we can render. We have chosen a small town to help us create a better environment, and in return we will offer our talents and skills to the local area. Tahlequah has a population of twelve thousand, plus a state university with five thousand students, and is a summer recreational area for Oklahoma. What more can one desire than to live in peace with God and humanity?"

Carol points out that as Mother Earth leaves the Piscean Age and enters the Aquarian Age, we too are in transit and must learn to live in a different way in the New Age. "We do not want a community so defined and rigid that it is our parent and we become dependent and weak," she explains. "We want a community that encourages growth, a supportive structure that encourages everyone in it, so that we can rejoice in each other's progress, and as each develops he or she can feel free to leave and start other communities. We want a place where New Age teachers can train, and where we can produce crops, because food will be a problem in the next twenty years. We have to work with and for humanity."

An important part of Carol's ministry has been counseling the terminally ill and the bereaved of all faiths, and she has worked with Dr. Elisabeth Kubler-Ross, the author-psychiatrist, in this endeavor. She has also been in touch with Dr. Kenneth Ring, a psychology professor at the University of Connecticut, who has been conducting studies on the remarkable alteration of personalities and ideals of individuals who have had near-death experiences.

Carol Parrish, in a letter to me, wrote: "It appears to me that Walk-ins may be the ones coming in to form the nucleus of communities, groups, or whatever, and then to form the networking needed to change our society. As we see so many sincere small groups form and then link themselves together, do you believe many of the focal-point persons are Walk-ins? Ruth, it seems to me that as New Age students study ideas about the externalization of the Hierarchy, or said another way, the disciples of the Christ coming forward, we should link the idea of beings using bodies already built, rather than having to go through the entire birth process. If there are to be major traumas for our society soon, it would seem likely that certain workers would come in through available doors to help guide humanity. I believe that few persons at the present time link the Walk-ins and the 'externalization of the Hierarchy' together, yet I see it that way."

I asked the Guides to tell me something of the previous lives of this remarkable Walk-in, and they replied: "Carol Parrish is a fine person with enormous potential, as her leadership is of high quality and she has the charisma to influence others in the right direction. The village project may not be an immediate success in terms of the numbers moving there, because of the deflated housing industry, but she will instill ideas that will have far-reaching results in self-help and mutual cooperation.

"Her predecessor in that body was afraid of her shadow, subservient to her husband and others, but with the transition the new Carol began to reach out for new understandings and investigate the world of the spirit, of which she had become aware in previous earth lives. In one former lifetime she was a princess in Arabia when it was near to the dawn of the present civilization, and in another she was a follower of Florence Nightingale, assisting in the care of the sick and wounded in the Crimea. She combines many talents brought forward from previous incarnations, and she will assume strong leadership in the difficult years ahead."

CHAPTER X
EDWARD HAGER

Early in 1982 I received a letter from a reader living in York, Pennsylvania, which began: "Over the past year I have been acquiring your various books relating to your contact with the Guides. To say the least, your writings have made a profound difference in my thinking and my life, as well as that of my wife's." It went on to say that four years previously he had been "in dire straits with a drinking problem, lack of employment, and seemingly no place to turn for help, when for the first time I really prayed to a Power greater than myself and meant it.

"At that moment I actually felt and heard unseen beings, like the guardian angels you have written about," he continued, "and they directed me to Alcoholics Anonymous and then to your book *A World Beyond*. I agree completely with Arthur Ford's witty comments on his battle with the bottle, and how he saw his past records once he had crossed into the spirit plane. In other words, do as much as you can to improve yourself in this world, so that faster progress can be made when you cross over. AA has been of immeasurable aid, but your writings have been of even more assistance to soothe a troubled mind and renew a worn spirit."

The letter detailed his vast improvement in the intervening years since licking his drinking problem; and because the late medium Arthur Ford had been an AA member, and was the primary contributor to *A World Beyond* after he passed into spirit, I thought that Arthur might appreciate knowing that he was still helping reformed alcoholics. I therefore mentioned the letter from Edward C. Hager to the Guides, before commencing my morning meditation, and after the automatic writing ceased, I read the following: "Hager is a Walk-in and will be surprised and gratified to learn of it, as it will explain much of what has happened to him recently. Tell him."

I did not know whether the man from York had even heard of Walk-ins, since he did not mention *Strangers Among Us* in his letter, but I dutifully followed instructions, and shortly thereafter received a long-distance call from Ed Hager, saying that he was delighted with the news, but not particularly surprised. He had indeed read my book about Walk-ins, and too many alterations had occurred within him to believe that he was the same entity who used to humiliate his family and friends by his drunken behavior.

I asked if he would be willing to tell me about his experiences for the book I was currently writing, and he gladly agreed. In a lengthy letter he wrote to say that he was born July 21, 1929, to a dentist and his wife in a suburb of Pittsburgh. An only child, he was somewhat introverted, and would go out of his way to avoid fights or strife during his boyhood. Then, while serving a tour of duty with the armed services overseas, he discovered liquor, "and on the way back on a troopship from Europe I had the 'shakes' from withdrawal symptoms; and my continued use of alcohol during periods of depression, or from actual or 'manufactured' problems, caused me no end of troubles.

"During this period I started college (the University of Pittsburgh) in night school, and stuck with it for eleven years to get my degree," he recounted. "I married in 1955, and we were blessed with two sons, while I moved up the ladder at United States Steel Corporation to middle-management level. Then I quit and went into sales."

Ed Hager said that for several of those years he had managed to stay on the wagon, but having convinced himself that he was not an alcoholic went back to the bottle, and in 1972 was divorced by his wife. Then, loaded with feelings of guilt, "I really started drinking heavily." Through a mutual friend he met his present wife, Mary, and before their marriage she succeeded in having him hospitalized to determine his mental condition, which was defined as manic-depressive.

He straightened up and they were married, but before long he was again hospitalized with the same diagnosis. "I was becoming a closet drinker, not wanting to have anyone around me or to socialize to any extent," he recalls ruefully. "My thinking had become totally warped. Everyone was in the wrong except me. I had excessive mood swings from fits of depression to high exhilaration. I thought everyone was out to get me—a classic alcoholic perversion. I kept kidding myself that I didn't really have a problem and could control my drinking, but I continued to go downhill: no job, my wife barely putting up with my roller-coaster moods, and my turning again and again to the bottle for solace and not finding it."

Finally he was "placed in the tank" of the hospital's mental ward. "I can remember that first night vividly, as all my fears, guilts, and gross behavior came back to haunt me," he wrote. "I thought the top of my head was literally going to blow off, and I cried out to God—not to save me—but to take me away forever. I did not want to continue to live. I wanted out! Perhaps at this time some potential Walk-ins were evaluating me to decide whether I was worth the time and trouble of saving. I had a slow but steady recovery, but kept nipping at Demon Rum until I actually became violent in March of 1978.

"Late one night I was alone and swearing to myself that I would never drink again. Then I turned my eyes inward on my true self and cried aloud,

"God, help me. Help me to see the light and find the right road. I can't go on."

He apparently passed out, but the next morning the road lay open before him. He attended a meeting of Alcoholics Anonymous, and "from that day on, one day at a time, I have not touched alcohol." He sensed an immediate alteration in his feelings about people, objects, life, and himself. He found a selling job, and when an opportunity arose he went into business for himself, founding a company in York that specializes in urethane spray foam and coatings.

He and his wife, Mary, together enrolled in an Alpha Awareness course, to which he feels that he was guided by an "inner voice," and he says that the "concentration, meditation, belief in a Power greater than ourselves, and the quiet but firm direction from our inner selves" enormously benefitted them. He then felt "directed" to pick up a copy of *A World Beyond* at a secondhand bookstore, and "from that moment on I finally found the answers to my many questions, and it ignited my quest for more knowledge, as if some unseen being is directing my steps to search further and deeper into the mysteries of life, life after death, and beyond. Reincarnation has always been a strong feeling of mine, but the view of your Guides has strengthened me in this belief."

Describing his altered attitudes, Hager said, "It is not for me to go around preaching to everyone at every chance I get, but by example or quiet words to my contemporaries to help ease their minds or guide them in some troublesome event, if only for the moment. When you are humbled to a great degree, as I was in the past, it makes your outlook quite different. My family has seen the change in me. Some people have commented on it, and others just smile and enjoy what they are experiencing. When your letter arrived with the news from the Guides that I was a Walk-in, I was not overly surprised. It explains so much to me."

Ed Hager's letter was eight typewritten pages long, and after perusing it I asked the Guides for comment. They wrote: "Hager made the crossover as he describes. His predecessor is here now, and remembers that with the final appeal to be saved from himself he was suddenly wafted out of the body and into spirit, where he rested for a time. He has since been reviewing his last lifetime with penitence and regret, but he is glad that he withdrew and will fight from this side to help those with alcohol problems to overcome them."

At my suggestion, Mary Hager wrote a delightful letter about the changes that she and others have observed in her husband since he became a Walk-in. "One of the most important ones is his ability to make sound, reasonable decisions now. Before, he would turn to someone else to do the reasoning, but watch out if you made the wrong decision for him! Then he would believe that you were someone who couldn't be trusted. In making repairs around the house, the job was formerly tackled in a very disorganized way, without any planning. He was a half-fast, half-fix-it man. Now he takes his time, and has just beautifully refinished an old high chair for our grandchildren.

"Ed was an offensive driver before, driving with

excessive speed and weaving in and out of traffic. Now he is a careful and considerate one. Being honest and able to tell the truth was another difficulty Ed had before. Now these qualities come easily for him. Egotism reigned supreme with the previous occupant of his body. When Ed entered a restaurant or other gathering of people, he would make sure that everyone knew he had arrived, and I would shrink with shame for him, but the grand entrances are now a thing of the past. We just arrive, and it's so pleasant this way!

"The former Ed's ego led to frequent family discord. He was always 'putting down' his two sons and my two daughters, trying to let them know how good and important he was. The children, as well as our friends, avoided him whenever they could, and seldom called, but now their visits are frequent and happy.

"Our neighbors have mentioned how changed he is, and at Christmastime my sister-in-law shook her head and marveled, 'Ed is so different. He's like a different person from a few years ago.' How true! We have not yet mentioned the word Walk-in to anyone, but the altered ego is so evident! When we took the awareness course, Ed was able to reach his alpha state much quicker than most of us, and to achieve remarkable results with a psychic detection project that was a part of the course. I'm sure he would not have been able to do that with the scatterbrain mind he had before."

Mary said she has often asked herself why she did not end the relationship with Ed before their marriage, when there were so many unpleasant happenings. "Shortly after our marriage, things deteriorated to an intolerable level, but I stayed on. There must have been some reason for it. I don't know the reason, except that I now feel so fortunate in having a Walk-in for a husband. I can honestly say to him, 'You're not the man I married,' and we kid about this, because he is now one of the most understanding people I know."

I asked the Guides for any final comments, and they wrote: "The original Ed Hager is a good example of a soul who, after addiction to alcohol, wishes to leave his body and start over again in a future life without the handicap of that addiction. There are many of them. Some of these withdraw during drunken bouts, and a new soul steps in to put the affairs in order, before using the circumstances and the body and mind to undertake projects for the good of mankind. The present Ed Hager is now finding that path to serve humanity."

CHAPTER XI

JANE POTTLE

Throughout the long years of our association, the Guides have repeatedly stressed that there is no such thing as an accident. Everything that happens is part of the divine plan, and how we react with our own free will to situations determines whether they help or hinder our spiritual progress. My encounter with Jane Pottle, which some would label accidental, is a case in point.

Like most authors, I customarily make a promotional television-radio tour to various cities when each of my books is first published. After appearances on the West Coast, the fall of 1979 found me in New York City, where, among others, I was booked for a daytime TV talk-show called *Midday Live,* which has audience participation. Since *Strangers Among Us* had only recently reached the bookstores, Bill Boggs, the TV host, asked me to describe the concept of Walk-ins, and I explained the process by which high-minded souls are permitted to enter an adult body if the occupant wishes to return to spirit or is unable to keep the physical body alive because of a clinical death or near-death experience.

When Bill Boggs opened the program to questions from the studio audience, a motherly looking, middle-aged woman arose and exclaimed, "Now I know what has happened to my daughter. She died for two minutes on the operating table, and this daughter I have now is a totally different personality. I feel that I hardly know her."

I asked where her daughter lives, and she replied, "She's sitting right here beside me." At her nudge, an embarrassed young woman stood up and said, "We came here today because we thought the subject was going to be astrology. I'm an astrologer."

The TV host registered surprise at this comment, but several others in the audience simultaneously called out, "That's right. Last week they announced that today's program would be about astrology."

I never learned how the mix-up in the announcement occurred. All I know is that Jane Pottle would not otherwise have been at the studio that day, and except for that "chance" encounter might not yet realize that she is occupying a body that previously belonged to another. And oddly enough, she is now no longer interested in astrology.

After the TV show I spoke briefly with Jane, before rushing to the airport for my next flight to Boston, and asked her to write me about her experience. By the time I returned home to Washington, Jane had obtained a copy of *Strangers Among Us*, had easily accepted the concept of Walk-ins as applying to herself, and was ready to tell me her story. I therefore asked the Guides about Jane, and was told by them that she was indeed a Walk-in, although she had not yet found her purpose.

At the time of our first meeting, Jane had been a Walk-in for only six months, but we have had frequent communication during the nearly three years since, and this is her story:

Jane Ann Buddington and Dean Smiley Pottle were married in 1977, and shortly thereafter moved from Connecticut to Tucson, Arizona, in search of clean air and year-round sunshine. Dean went to work as a contractor, and Jane as a part-time waitress and astrologer. She also became involved with the Great White Brotherhood, an ancient sect that is interested in psychic development.

Sunday, March 11, 1979, was a beautiful, sunny day, and Jane was driving to church in her yellow Karmann Ghia sports car along a broad boulevard, when a white Cadillac driven by a man in his eighties suddenly pulled out from a side street directly into her path. A crash was inevitable, and Jane's head went through the windshield. When she regained consciousness after a few minutes, she discovered that her legs were trapped by the smashed car, and her breathing was labored and irregular.

A crowd had gathered, along with the police, and the car doors were so crushed from the impact that they could not be opened. "But suddenly a nun was sitting beside me in the passenger seat," Jane recalls. "She was holding my hand, telling me to breathe slowly, and that help was on the way. She also wiped blood from my face and nostrils, so that I could get my breath. I was praying, and mentally calling for help from the Archangel Michael and my brothers and sisters of the Great White Brotherhood. Then paramedics arrived and broke open the door on my side of the car. They gave me some kind of drug, cut off all of my clothing, and asked whom they should notify. I remember telling them to reach into my purse for a card that told where Dean was working that day. Oddly enough, it was the first time in months that I had bothered to jot down Dean's phone number at work. I still couldn't move my legs, so the paramedics lifted me onto a stretcher and into the ambulance. I was wide awake and coherent, but the nun had vanished, and no one was able to locate her afterward, although other bystanders said they had seen her, and the police were looking for witnesses to the collision. Whether she was an angel who had materialized to help or a human being, I don't know."

The hospital was only a block away, and as Jane was being rolled down the corridor she saw her husband racing along to keep up with the stretcher. Dean was able to reach her parents by telephone, and they hastily caught a plane at LaGuardia Airport for the flight to Tucson. Jane says of this frantic period, "My operation lasted from three P.M. until eight P.M. at the Tucson Medical Center, and my doctors said that at seven thirty P.M. I died for two minutes. I am told that at that exact time my mother became hysterical on the airplane, and had to be subdued by my father and the stewardesses."

Jane says that she remembers nothing of the five-hour operation, except that at one point she seemed to be viewing the doctors and nurses from above, "floating aloft and trying to decide whether or not to return to my body. The decision was a difficult one. The accident had torn off my nose and broken my pelvis. The body was racked with pain because of the broken ribs that had punctured my heart and lungs. The doctors say it was a miracle that I survived."

She recalls similar out-of-the-body experiences during the month that she spent in the intensive care unit, before her removal to the respiratory wing of the hospital for another month of treatments.

"I became psychically aware," she says, "knowing when my particular doctors would turn the corridor leading toward my room. While out of the body I watched doctors and nurses working on other patients in various parts of the hospital, and I can remember the feeling of warmth, security, protection, and encouragement that I would receive at those times from discarnates. Death became a wonderful feeling, and life a burden with an awesome sense of purpose. I remember having a long conversation during this period in the intensive care unit with a woman I knew from the Great White Brotherhood, who told me that the membership was praying for my recovery, but I later learned that she had not visited me. She did come to my home afterward, during my convalescence.

"I was told by the doctors that they did not know

why I had lived through such an ordeal, but I knew why. I wanted to live. I was no longer the 'old Jane' who would have given up easily at the thought of insurmountable hardships. I believe the actual changeover of egos came gradually, as 'I' came to Jane in the hospital, offering my help, and she gladly accepted a temporary relief from pain until the changeover was completed. It was a voluntary relationship, which proved beneficial for both of us."

The feeling of Jane's that it was a gradual changeover is eerily like that of the Walk-in whom I called Laura in *Strangers Among Us*. Laura is able to recall that she "took turns" occupying the body of the discouraged girl who had a death wish, until the transferral of egos was finally effected. It was as if both Jane and Laura were trying out the bodies to learn how to manage them, before taking the final plunge.

Jane says that during this transition period she had several dreams in which she was offered a choice of living at the ethereal or physical level, and that in some of them she was conversing with crowds of spirits and human beings who could not contact each other, except through her. Her most jolting experience was awakening one day and "seeming to feel earth gravity for the first time, although I had a dim memory of how it felt to eat and walk."

"My personality since then has changed drastically," she declares, "and close friends and relatives frequently comment on it. People who knew me before viewed me as a too-emotional, overly sensitive person who had barely graduated from high school, and could not even finish one semester of college work. Since the accident I have a new sense of purpose, a mission to accomplish, and a sword of strength which I believe to be a gift from the Archangel Michael. I have no fear of death, and my emotions are easily controlled. I don't become personally involved in others' complaints and personal piques. Even though I sense a mission, I do not clearly know yet what it is, except that it requires higher education."

In discussing this altered attitude, she made some interesting observations: "The old Jane was an outstanding cook who prepared delicious vegetarian dishes. She was an astrologer. She was also involved in politics and tried many times, without success, to finish courses in political science. Now, as a Walk-in, I am in my second year of pre-medical studies at Sacred Heart University in Connecticut, with an A average. The old Jane received a D in high school chemistry and dropped out of the course. Last year I received the Most Outstanding Chemistry Student of the Year award at my university. The new Jane, to my husband's chagrin, can no longer cook well, concentrating mainly on fast foods. And I am no longer interested in practicing astrology or making campaign speeches. What I *am* interested in are my studies in biology and in finding ways of easing people's physical and emotional stresses when in traumatic situations or when facing death. I also have become quite practical, investing most of my insurance settlement in business ventures. I've gotten rid of the faddish clothes I wore before, and have bought a much more conservative wardrobe that suits my new attitude and life-style."

Jane says that her relationship with others has markedly changed. People she used to dislike she now enjoys, whereas many of her former friends now turn her off. She and Dean moved back to Easton, Connecticut, after her miracle of survival, and he now works in a chemistry laboratory testing foods for levels of contaminants, and for their nutritional content. Jane is currently leaning toward a career as a physician, although she says that the 'old Jane' would never have considered being a doctor.

"The old Jane was happier with less responsibility," she explains, "but since the accident I see the importance of having good doctors. Really good doctors are needed in the world, and I became familiar with healing techniques during my two months in the hospital. I feel that I can be helpful in this field, and that I will be needed if and when catastrophe comes. The old Jane was always trying to 'find herself,' but that is no longer a problem. I am happier and more content now, and I spend less time on 'finding myself' than on 'doing.' I believe that what I am doing is along the right path, and accomplishment is the way."

While writing this chapter, I asked the Guides for further comment and they wrote: "As we said earlier, Jane Pottle has not yet found her true niche, and she will become more alert and helpful when she settles into her real mission, which is to assist others both financially and spiritually, as a leader of study groups and as a public speaker. She will attain recognition before long."

Jane's husband had occasionally telephoned me during the past two years, and I asked him what differences he had noticed in his wife since the transferral of egos. He said that for one thing the former Jane was more flexible, and they used to make decisions together, "but now she seems to make up her mind without me, with a singleness of purpose.

"Since the accident Jane has had a compulsion to contribute to needy causes, including many organizations devoted to the welfare of animals," Dean continued. "She donated a movie screen to her science department at school, anonymously. She is now always looking for any excuse to give money to her family and friends, particularly those she feels are especially deserving of it. She really has a new sense of courage in undertaking tasks she would not have considered before. The summer after the accident Jane started going to jai-alai to gamble with her parents, and did so well that she decided to use her earnings to go back to school. It was as if she were meant to have that money for education, and at the time it was the only way we could have afforded it. The first year of college Jane would study to the exclusion of everything else—all day, evenings, sometimes all night long, and certainly all weekend long. I've never seen anyone with such perseverance."

I asked the Guides why Jane, who is now twenty-six years old, is willing to undertake the long years of study required to qualify as a physician, and they replied: "In a previous life Jane was a very beneficial person who aided others. She began that life as a street waif in London, and used to seek out those in need of assistance. As she grew to maturity she became so helpful that when she passed into spirit she desired to return as quickly as possible, in order to be of even more assistance to others this time around. That is why she chose to come back into an adult body, to save time. She will find her true niche when she accepts this pledge that she made before entering the body of one who was unable to maintain it after the accident. But of course, there are no accidents."

CHAPTER XII
SEATTLE SURPRISE

It is strange how life works its little ironies. Or is it all part of a predestined plan? The trips I take for personal pleasure often leave little but a blurred memory, whereas those I am most reluctant to make seem to have constructive, long-reaching results.

In a weak moment, early in 1981, I had promised Fawcett Books that when the paperback edition of *Strangers Among Us* appeared I would make a limited tour for them, to appear on some television and radio talk-shows. At the time I had no intention of ever writing another book, and Fawcett had been good to me in collecting all of my soft-cover editions in the psychic field under one umbrella.

As publication date approached, I deeply regretted my decision. By February 1982 I was writing this book, and not only are such promotional trips extremely exhausting, but I desperately needed those three weeks to work on the manuscript. Fawcett was understandably holding me to my commitment, and the Guides were highly unsympathetic with my despair. Don't worry about it, they kept advising at our morning sessions. You will be glad that you went.

There go those darned Guides again, I thought mulishly. Since they can effortlessly flit around to wherever they want to go, they seem to have forgotten the toll that such trips take on a physical body. They don't even have to be concerned with earth time anymore, whereas I have a May first deadline.

But how right the Guides proved to be! Or perhaps they arranged the whole thing, because I found myself practically stumbling over Walk-ins wherever I went. In retrospect it seems rather a joke on myself that at a small seated dinner in Seattle, three of the eight guests were Walk-ins and I didn't even know it. But I do recall the warmth and *simpatico* of the gathering that evening at the attractive residence of Shirlee Teabo, who is a columnist for the Seattle *Post-Intelligencer* and director of The Sixth Sense, an organization that sponsors seminars featuring lecturers in the psychic field.

I had briefly met Shirlee at a seminar several years ago in Oklahoma, when she interviewed me for her column. The encounter seemed unimportant at the time, but how times change! When she learned that I would be in Seattle during the West Coast leg of my Fawcett tour, she telephoned long-distance to ask if I would address her group; and if I had not remained over in Seattle an extra day to do so, I would not have met a number of fascinating Walk-ins who have greatly contributed to this book.

As William Cowper so aptly phrased it two centuries ago, "God moves in a mysterious way, His wonders to perform."

My speech that day in Seattle was principally about Walk-ins, and when I asked if anyone in the audience of some three hundred people believed that he or she knew one, I was surprised to see approximately fifty hands go up. Never had I met with such an overwhelming response to that question. But my surprise turned to astonishment when, on my return home, the Guides told me that at least seven of those with whom I had personally talked in Seattle are Walk-ins, although unaware of it. "It may seem odd to you that so many are working in that area," they wrote, "but the Northwest and California are gathering places for many of these New Age disciples."

I also had my comeuppance from another source. When by long-distance I excitedly told Michael (my Walk-in friend whom I discussed at length in *Strangers Among Us*) that he would be surprised at how many Walk-ins I had found on my tour, he commented wryly, "My only surprise is that *you* are surprised."

Shirlee Teabo's guests at the dinner party for me that memorable evening included her mother, her sister Jacquie Witherrite, and three friends, one of them her co-worker in The Sixth Sense, Barbara Easton, and another an attractive Englishman named David Hutton. It was an interesting group, and on observing Shirlee's husband, Robert Ranjel, I thought that if I were a Hollywood director I would cast the tall, handsome gentleman in the role of an aristocratic Spanish don.

The conversation turned naturally to the subject of my address earlier that day, and several of those present remarked that if anyone met all of the qualifications for a Walk-in it was Shirlee's husband. "Bob has never said an unkind word about anyone," and "He is so helpful to everyone, without seeking any credit for himself" were only two of the many comments. Robert Ranjel gave a slow smile, but depreciated the compliments and said that as far as he knew, he was not a Walk-in.

David Hutton, the Britisher who now lives in Portland, Oregon, looked on with lively interest and sparkling eyes, but said little. Afterward Barbara Easton gave me a lift in her car, and enroute back to my hotel mentioned a near-death experience nineteen years earlier that had totally altered the direction of her life.

I flew back to Washington the next day, and after a good night's sleep prepared to resume my morning sessions with the Guides. I had met a number of people on the tour who thought that they might be Walk-ins, and since I never rely on my own hunches in so important a matter, I typed a list of their names for the Guides, before beginning my meditation. I included the names of Robert Ranjel and Barbara Easton, although I was not particularly expectant. Three times out of four the Guides will write: "A fine soul, but not a Walk-in."

They proceeded to do just that with a number of

the names on my list that morning, but they definitely stated that both Robert and Barbara are Walkins, and they later supplied the information that David Hutton and four others who had spoken with me in Seattle were also occupying bodies that had originally belonged to others. They told me a little bit about them, and at their direction I relayed the information to those concerned.

Their response was not long in coming. All were surprised, but none was shocked, and several of them readily agreed to let me tell their stories, which now follow.

CHAPTER XIII
ROBERT RANJEL

I knew nothing about my tall, good-looking host, Bob Ranjel, except that during the dinner party he remarked that his original name had been Roberto Gonzales, and his wife, Shirlee, murmured that his early years had not been easy ones. Later, in asking my Guides about him, I therefore phrased the question: "Please tell me if Roberto Gonzales, now called Robert Ranjel, is a Walk-in."

After my usual period of meditation, the writing began, and when it ceased I read the following: "As to Roberto, he is a Walk-in in an unusual way, for the original spirit left the body at an early age and Robert was transformed into a wonderful, loving, giving, caring person. He was barely into his teens when the bitterness of his existence prompted the original occupant of that body to withdraw, and this high-minded soul entered to take its place; for he saw the vast potential of rising from the slums to set an example for other young people in the neighborhood, and to overcome any obstacle in achieving a perfection of spirit. Ask him to recall that time when he was so discouraged and low in spirits that he prayed for release. He will remember that period and the emergence of such energy, faith, and willpower that his life was revolutionized."

I was rather astonished at this message, since the Guides had previously indicated that Walk-ins enter *adult* bodies, to save time in commencing their projects to help mankind. I also felt some embarrassment in forwarding it to Shirlee and Bob, because it seemed to belittle his background. I need not have worried. The Guides knew what they were about, as soon became apparent. I sent a copy of the message to Bob, and also a list of questions in the event that he was willing to be included in this book.

Shortly thereafter I received a letter from Shirlee, saying that Bob, for the first time, was "really reviewing his life, and it's like a catharsis of his soul." She said the revelation of his being a Walk-in had already changed his life, and she added: "I'm not surprised that he is a Walk-in, as I know how special and good he is, not just here at home but in all areas of his life."

Enclosed was a tape recording that Bob had made in answer to my many questions, and as I listened to his beautifully modulated voice recounting the pathos of his childhood, I had a sizable lump in my throat. He said that he was born on a farm in Kansas, on May 13, 1938, the youngest of six children. At the age of three he moved with his family to Toppenish, Washington, where his grandmother also shared their tiny cottage, and the boys slept four to a bed on a pull-out sofa.

His father worked at a farm labor camp, in the hop fields, and he recalls that "there was a lot of love for awhile. We had two dogs and some kittens, and when there was money for coal we took our baths in a round tub beside the stove. My mother worked in a restaurant, and my dad was a drinking man who began coming home less and less frequently. We had no money for clothes and little for food, and I can remember my fear when Dad would come home late, in an angry mood, and begin arguing loudly with my mother. As time went on, he would come pounding on the windows and doors, demanding entry when he was drunk, and my sister and I would run in terror to a neighbor who had a telephone, to call the police, because we never knew at such times what he would do to my mother and grandmother and the kids.

"In the second and third grades, when other kids would ask what my father did for a living, I was bitterly ashamed. We were seeing him less and less, and we never knew where the rent money would come from. Our aunt Mary would sometimes ask us over to eat, knowing that we had no food and that my dad was taking another woman around."

Bob said that he used to scour the alleys for anything that would burn, to keep the stove going during the bitter winters, and that the happiest day he remembers was one Thanksgiving when there was a knock on the door, and someone had left a box of groceries on the front stoop. "We had had only a few bits of bread in the house," he recalls, "and I will never forget the box of chocolate-covered doughnuts that came in the box of groceries. Christmas was always a very painful time for us, and after the holidays the teacher would tell each of us in turn to come to the front of the classroom and tell what we got for Christmas. I still can barely endure Christmas music today. It reminds me too painfully of the embarrassment and humility of it all, because, of course, we had received nothing."

One of the most poignant parts of Bob's account concerns the family pets. "I was in the third grade, when we had to watch our little kittens die of starvation. At the same time our two dogs, whom we had loved for so many years, were taken away and put to death because we had no money to pay for their license or to feed them anymore. It made me feel very desperate, and it still troubles me a great deal that a choice had to be made between food for the kids and those two wonderful animals. But in every life there is pain."

Continuing, Bob said that toward the close of the sixth grade he was feeling particularly desperate and lonely. School authorities had finally discovered that he could not see very well, which caused difficulties with his studies, so they told him he would have to take the sixth grade over again.

"I remember going outside in an open area that night, looking up at the heavens, and longing to go 'home' again," he mused. "I can certainly relate to what the Guides said about praying for release. I was indeed praying for release from the degradation, the pain, the loneliness, and the hunger of it all. I vividly remember that prayer. Then, as I was standing there, I suddenly felt myself uplifted toward the heavens, and I was rising higher and higher. I felt very light and extremely happy, just like I was going home again. With it all came a marvelous sense of release."

Bob does not know how long that experience of soaring lasted, but he does know that his life completely changed. "I immediately became aware that the kids I had been running around with were going in a different direction than I should be going," he said. "I knew it was not the place that I should be going, and of the four kids who were my closest friends until that moment of alteration, one has since been killed and the others are serving prison sentences.

"After that experience in the open area, I discovered that I could see the end results of what was taking place. I felt that I should love and cherish those around me, because we would be on earth such a short time. I even felt forgiveness for my dad, and a lot of love and compassion for him. I had no place for hatred in my life, nor do I now, because even when I was that thirteen-year-old in the sixth grade I realized that if I hated someone I'd have less space and time available for love, and my life would be too short to hate anyone."

The lad who had been put back a grade in school now found that "even older kids were seeking me out for counseling about their problems—problems they wouldn't talk about even to their peers or their parents. They looked up to me. From the sixth grade on I knew intuitively that life was a continuing cycle. I believed in reincarnation and UFOs. It was a knowing! It was also a searching for everything that I could learn about the world beyond our five senses and about past lives. I found that I was in no position to judge others. Until I had walked their path in life, I could not judge anybody. I have yet to meet anyone since then with whom I can't get along."

After graduation from high school in 1957, Bob went into the navy for two years, serving on the admiral's staff at the U.S. base in Kodiak, Alaska. Then he worked for a time at a cannery in Toppenish, before getting a job with a chemical plant in Seattle. It was while employed there that he began a concentrated search to prove the validity of reincarnation and psychic phenomena. He attended a professional school of hypnosis in order to conduct hypnotic regressions into past lives, took the Silva Mind Control course, and devoured books in the psychic field.

"I read your books, Ruth, and it was just like a refresher course," he mused. "They confirmed what I had always felt since the sixth grade, and gave me a better understanding of what is taking place. I wanted to find a good psychic, and when a friend at work said he was taking his mother to one and invited me to go along, I met Shirlee. She was that psychic, and I became a buffer for her, because I feel that she has a great destiny and a great deal to do for the betterment of mankind. I must help her anyway that I can. We were married seven months after the day that we met, and I assist her and Barbara Easton with their seminars. I also do hypnotic regressions and give psychic palm readings at clubs. I think I've found my proper place, because it gives me a position from which I can help people and give them options for the direction in which they should go. I have a lesson to learn. Everyone does, and before I bring my clients out of hypnosis I always let them know that they have a lesson to learn and that the sooner they get on with it the sooner they will get into the flow. Love is what it's all about."

I asked Bob about his name change, and he explained, "The name Gonzales was never really a part of me. It's not the new me. My grandmother's name was Anna Baron Ranjel, and that surname fits the new me much more comfortably."

After listening to his moving tape, I prodded the Guides for more information about Bob and Shirlee. "Roberto is one of the finest of the fine," they began. "In a previous lifetime he was a high-ranking dignitary of the Catholic Church in Spain, and afterward felt that he had no right to have found life so easy and rewarding in that incarnation. He therefore entered the body of that little boy who so desperately wanted to leave it. He chose a Spanish family in a slum as a fitting place from which to achieve grace, and work to raise the levels of others. Such a good, good soul! Shirlee is not a Walk-in, but a highly developed soul who in previous lives studied metaphysics and soul development, and is well equipped to carry on in this lifetime as an instructor in spiritual development and soul orientation."

Later I asked them to tell me something of Xan,

Shirlee's remarkable guide, about whom she has written several articles in the Seattle *Post-Intelligencer,* and they replied: "She knew him in a Persian life when he was her consort on the throne. Both were members of the nobility and extremely devoted one to the other. A continuing relationship."

Persian nobility! No wonder, I thought with a smile, that Shirlee's beautiful table that evening in Seattle was set with gold-rimmed plates and golden tableware.

I told the Ranjels by telephone what the Guides had written, and Shirlee exclaimed, "So that's why everyone seems to come to Bob with their problems, ever since he was a boy! It's probably a continuation of his work as a Catholic priest in the confessional."

Bob, in his quiet way, commented, "I was baptized and reared as a Catholic in this present life, but I never felt comfortable there, and after my experience in the sixth grade I refused to go to church. I have always felt closer to the Creator walking in the woods or looking at a newborn baby. This certainly helps me put a lot of pieces of the puzzle together, but I wish the Guides would tell you whether I'm moving along in the right direction."

I did pose that question to the Guides, and they wrote: "He *is* going in the right direction. He will be of great assistance in counseling other Walk-ins, and those with problems in finding themselves. Let him take heart from the fact that his influence is spreading in the area, and that he will be a leader during these stormy decades as a voice of reason and calm.

He knew Shirlee in a Persian and a Turkish life. They are akin in many ways, and his calming and reasoning attitude is helping her to find the right pathway as well. Before long he will branch out into a counseling service in which she too will play a part."

CHAPTER XIV
BARBARA EASTON

Barbara Easton is so poised and attractive that it is difficult to visualize her having undergone the harrowing near-death experience she described to me that memorable evening after Shirlee Teabo's dinner party in Seattle. Actually, the Guides say that she is not the same entity as the frightened, intimidated young woman who lay dying in a hospital bed nearly two decades ago. When I queried them about Barbara, they wrote: "She is indeed a Walk-in and will continue to soar above her previous heights. Do get in touch with her."

I therefore wrote to Barbara, asking numerous questions about her life before and after the apparent transfer of egos, and she promptly replied: "Your letter of yesterday has me in a whirl. I'm not sure whether I'm pleased to find that I am a Walk-in, but of one thing I'm sure. It was a surprise! As I told you when we talked, I have increasingly felt an urgency to do some things on a larger scale than I have been doing. Now I feel compelled to get started." She enclosed a tape recording to answer my questions, and in it she expressed some astonishment at how "painful" it had been for her to review the life of her predecessor in that body.

Barbara said that she was born on a farm in Iowa, and has two older sisters and a younger brother. "My dad was a farmer," she continued, "and I remember best his sense of humor and how he used to play the guitar and sing in the evenings. Music to this day is an important part of my life. My mother was a dedicated mother. She sewed all of our clothes, canned all the food, and, in general, was a typical midwestern farmer's wife. We attended the Primitive Baptist Church regularly, and were heavily involved with aunts, uncles, cousins, and grandparents. We had little money, but were a reasonably happy family, although I was rather a loner, who liked to be off by myself.

"When I was thirteen we moved to Moses Lake, Washington, and everything changed drastically. Mother went to work, and my dad started drinking. Family life was gone. We girls all went to work. Moses Lake was a boom town, so there was lots of money but little direction. I liked school, but family life continued to deteriorate, and at fifteen I ran away and got married. By the age of eighteen I had three babies and a most unhappy marriage. That marriage was my introduction to a heavily organized religion. My in-laws lived next door and kept me scared to death. Everything was a sin, and we had to go to church three times a week. My husband was a heavy drinker and girl chaser, but his family's answer to all my problems was that if I didn't submit God would take my children. And those three children were the joy of my life! At twenty I obtained a divorce, which was shocking to my family, and spent the next two years working and raising the babies. Then I married a man eight years older than myself, and had a fourth child.

"My husband was in construction, and we moved every few months. Ruth, I felt like we were poor white trash. It was like we were driving Cadillacs one day, and the next day living in the boxes they came in. It was a nightmare. We were existing in poverty, and while I was trying to find food for the children, I was carefully keeping those conditions from my family, because I was too proud to let them know how I was living. There were some good times, when we would play the guitar and sing together, but there were so many bad times!"

Barbara says that in 1958 she went to work for the Sarah Coventry Jewelry Company, which assigned her to Seattle, but after a few months she became desperately ill. "The next three years were horrible," she recalls with a sigh. "I had ulcerative colitis, and the pain was constant. The marriage deteriorated, work was scarce, and we were at the poverty level. Then my appendix ruptured, and I almost died. Finally I went back to work out of sheer desperation, but still had the colitis. Then on July 26, 1963, I was rushed to the hospital in the middle of the night. Surgery was performed immediately, and again the following Monday, after which the doctor said, 'Barbara, we've done all we can.' At that time, living did not seem important anyway."

She recalls that two days later she was lying in bed, "with an IV in one arm, blood transfusion in the other arm, and tubes in my nose. I was terribly hot. One minute I was lying there in excruciating pain, and the next minute I was up at the ceiling level looking down at the woman in the bed. There was no fear at all. I seemed to know that if I went up higher I would never come back. I do not remember any sounds. I don't know how long I debated about it all. My one worry was about the children. Who would take care of them? Then I went higher and seemed to be talking to God about how I would live my life. Suddenly I floated into that body, as light as a feather, although I spent six more months in recuperation."

Barbara says that almost immediately after the floating experience she became aware of radical changes within herself. "I seemed to have an inner knowing. I knew that I was finally headed someplace. I was no longer a drifter, and within a year I obtained a divorce. I suddenly experienced tremendous energy, and I still have tons more of it than I need. I sleep only four or five hours a night and wake up thinking, What wonderful thing is going to happen today? I feel like everyday is a birthday party. Since that near-death experience I'm much better organized. I'm a much better housekeeper.

Before, I felt no control over my life; then suddenly I felt so good about life and about others. I experienced such compassion and such a delightful feeling of being in the flow! I continued to work for the jewelry company for fifteen years, and became very successful in that career, but the children have remained a focal point in my life, and have turned out to be very special people."

Barbara believes that if one word could describe what has transpired since that fateful day when she apparently entered the body of a dying woman, it would be *direction*.

"I don't hear voices," she explains. "It's just a 'knowing' that is given to me. Since that day in the hospital I have felt a great urgency to help others. I became an avid reader of books on Eastern religions and self-development. I became aware that I was extremely psychic, and I began giving readings to help others discover themselves. But I most enjoy lecturing at seminars where I can reach a wider range of people. That's where my work seems to be taking me now, because lately the one-to-one readings appear to be draining me, and causing severe pain in my forehead where the Third Eye is said to be located. Perhaps that is a signal that I should be reaching out to more people, rather than doing the individual counseling."

I asked the Guides for further comment on the new Barbara who took over the body of that poverty-stricken, pain-wracked young woman, and they wrote: "In a previous lifetime she was a nurse who founded a teaching order, and was instrumental in establishing certain procedures that are still used today in many nursing establishments. She was a caring, seeking, loving person, and when the strictures of the church became intolerable she set up her own establishment outside the religious order. That is why she feels restricted by orthodoxy within the church, and why she left it to seek her own means of direct contact with the Creator, both within and without. She will soon set up a counseling-teaching service, and will find her way again to directed work that will benefit many more than she can now reach. She is on her way."

The Guides added that in one life Barbara had been a Druze, which could help to explain her interest in the esoteric field, and in another was a highly respected housekeeper to nobility in England. Each of us is obviously a small part in each incarnation of a much more varied mosaic.

CHAPTER XV
DAVID HUTTON

Two adult friends could scarcely have experienced more dissimilar upbringings than the hunger-ridden slums that produced Robert Ranjel and the upper-class English background of David Hutton. Yet both became Walk-outs and were replaced in those bodies by enlightened souls who are dedicated to serving humanity. Both vividly feel the change within themselves, and the Guides have verified their inner promptings.

As previously related, I met David at the home of Shirlee Teabo and her husband, Robert Ranjel, and was impressed by his attractive appearance and unassuming demeanor, although we had little opportunity for conversation together. Afterward he wrote to me, saying that while he had no wish to draw attention to himself, he believes that he is a Walk-in because his goals and interests have so drastically altered in recent years.

"I used to be career-motivated, with a very good job that paid good money and with every intention of succeeding in the business world," he pointed out. "I was intellectually rather than spiritually inclined. In fact, I was rather condemning of religion. I had a lot of ego, a low boiling point, and flirtatious habits. I was a classic product of my upper-class English background, and thought myself superior to most.

"Now, by contrast, my sense of purposefulness to be of service to humankind is all-consuming. My circle of friends has completely changed, to the distress of my wife, as I really no longer have anything in common with them. I have become much more intuitive, and I have a great sense of awareness of what lies ahead and a clear idea of my role in the scheme of things, although there is no ego attached to this thinking. Just a desire to serve. My thoughts are concentrated almost entirely on the road ahead, and I regret time spent on material matters for today, although I recognize the need to provide for my family and assist them in every way. I write spiritual poetry, with no previous training or experience in that activity. People who knew me four or five years ago see the difference immediately, when they meet me now."

The Guides readily confirmed David's intuitive feeling that he is a different soul from the previous occupant of that body, and pointedly suggested that he try to recall the actual transferral "at a time not too long ago when he was in what could be called a trancelike sleep and exchanged places with the one that he is now." I relayed this message to David, and before long received a fascinating response. But before proceeding with that account, I would like to review the background of his predecessor and the memory patterns that he inherited when he stepped into the human role of David Hutton.

He was born December 15, 1946, in Ipswich, Suffolk County, England, to Stella Luxmore-Ball and Walter Morland Hutton, now a major general who rose through the British army to take command of all its armored divisions. David was only eighteen months old when he accompanied his parents to America, where his father was chief liaison officer for the British-U.S. armored divisions. Two years later they returned to England, and in 1953 moved to Jordan, where General Hutton served as chief of staff to Lieutenant General John Bagot Glubb, the legendary "Glubb Pasha" who commanded Jordan's Arab Legion. While there, little David became the playmate of Prince Hussan, younger brother of King Hussein of Jordan. This was shortly after the assassination of their father, King Abdullah.

From the ages of eight to thirteen, David was sent to a private boarding school called Horris Hill near Newbury, England, and after graduation enrolled at Haileybury College in Hartfordshire, the traditional training school for British military officers. But he spent his holidays in Aden, where his father, who wrote and spoke Arabic fluently, was responsible for the defense of the vast Arab lands from British

Somaliland through Muscat and the Trucial States to Kuwait. Major General Hutton, on his retirement, was named administrator of one of the colleges at Oxford University, and David lived with his family near Blenheim Palace, the birthplace of Sir Winston Churchill.

Here David takes up his story: "In the summer of 1969 I was working for a division of Dunlop Company Limited, but I was bored with the job, and my London social life had paled on me. I felt a great sense of restlessness and a need to break out of the mold. While on a training course for junior managers with Dunlop at Oxford University I ran into Peter Clegg, an old friend of my father's and the person who had initially interviewed me for Dunlop after I left Angers University in France. He was, of course, aware of my international background and of my fluency in French, so he found me a position in the International Division of Dunlop and sent me to Nigeria, which was in the process of concluding a bloody civil war. Life seemed suddenly challenging again."

This is the background of the "former" David Hutton, and we now skip to the day early last March when the present David received my letter containing the challenge from my Guides to "recall the actual transferral . . . during what could be called a trancelike sleep."

David later told me that he seemed unable to recall such an event, but spent a restless night, awakening in the predawn from an incredibly vivid dream in which he seemed to be looking down on a middle-aged man. "The man was very sick," he remembers with a shudder, "and through his deathly white sheen every vein and capillary was clearly showing beneath the skin. As I looked at the man I was fighting back my intensity of absolute grief, and a sense of hopelessness because I could not alleviate his condition. Then I suddenly realized to my horror that I was actually looking at our planet Earth. I awoke immediately and went downstairs to the family room, where I sat in total darkness, the vision of the man etched in my mind and tears in my eyes. I remember saying over and over again that I was absolutely determined to make whatever contribution I could to the curing of this planet's ills. I would not allow the planet to die. I became increasingly aware that all of my innermost thoughts about being here to make a significant contribution to the case of humankind were 'right on.' I was also assailed with the thought that I simply had to go to Seattle that day, for what reason I did not know; but I called Shirlee Teabo to tell her that I had this compulsion to make the long journey from Portland, Oregon to Seattle, Washington."

After seeing Shirlee for an hour and recounting the upsetting dream, he spent the rest of the evening with other friends. The next morning he saw Shirlee again to say good-bye, and received an intense surprise.

"In the course of our conversation," he said, "Shirlee told me that the previous evening she had had a visit with her Guide, Xan, and he told her that I became a Walk-in while in Africa, 'when I was driving in a jeep on a very bad road out in the bush country, and had an accident involving a truck. The previous entity left and I walked in.'

"You can well appreciate my intense astonishment at her words," David continued, "because it had never occurred to me to tell her about that incident. As she spoke, however, total clarity came to me, and I can now recount exactly what happened."

David then told me the previously mentioned facts about how he happened to go to Nigeria, and said that shortly after his arrival he was asked by his superior to go to Ibadan, one hundred miles north of Lagos, to help with a Dunlop promotion. "I left early and I remember feeling uneasy about making the trip, with a definite presentiment that something unpleasant was about to happen. The roads were in terrible condition due to the war, and contrary to the advice of my new colleagues I took a shorter route, rather than the longer and more traveled road. What I had apparently foreseen happened about seventy miles out. I do not remember anything about the accident and can only describe what appeared to have happened, based on the subsequent police report. Apparently I had just turned a corner when the prop shaft of an old truck carrying sugar from the refinery in Ibadan to Lagos broke, and the front end of the shaft fell into one of the many potholes that were two to three feet deep. The effect of this was to hurtle the truck out of control onto my vehicle, completely crushing my Land Rover. I was thrown clear, and the truck driver 'went for bush.'

"How long I was unconscious I do not know. All that I can remember is coming 'round with a kindly, elderly white man with white hair leaning over and assisting me. He said that he was a missionary who happened to be passing by, and he took me to the Ibadan Teaching Hospital. I counted myself very lucky that he happened along, because there was almost no traffic on that dreadful road. The missionary disappeared, and I never saw or heard from him again. I wrote to him in care of the address that he left at the hospital, but received no reply. The police also tried to find him to make a statement about the accident, but were unable to locate his whereabouts. It was as if he had never existed!"

It is within the realm of possibility that the white-haired man did indeed materialize from spirit, to assist the Walk-out to depart painlessly and the Walk-in to enter, because the Guides say that spirit assistance is always required to effect the actual transition. And anyone familiar with Eastern religions has read similar accounts of Ascended Masters who can become visible when circumstances require, to perform earthly missions.

David quickly recovered from his cuts and bruises, and the next year married the daughter of an American diplomat in Nigeria, by whom he now has two children. In 1973 he left Dunlop to develop a West African market for Abbott Laboratories, a Chicago-based firm, and two years later was offered excellent opportunities to work with two major companies in their international divisions. "Instead, I turned them down in favor of an obscure computer software company in Portland, Oregon, because I felt that it was the course of action I had to take," he said, "even though on the surface it was outside the area where my skills and expertise lay."

After moving to Portland, he for the first time came into contact with people who were interested in metaphysical and psychic studies, and his own abilities in that field rapidly began to flower. "The bottom line is that I now know what I am here to do," he declared. "I have a feel for the broad tapestry of events to come and my role in those events, although the only uncertainty is how my particular role will unfold. My predecessor was a Sagittarian, but since my Walk-in birth on February 3, 1970, I am an Aquarian, and am no longer confused by the fact that for some years after the event, my actions continued to reflect the predominant characteristics of the previous occupant. You see, I am convinced that my predecessor did not walk out from boredom, but that it was a prearranged event prior to the birth of the first entity in this body."

David is not alone in believing that many of these exchanges of ego are a fulfillment of prior promises. In *Strangers Among Us* the Guides pointed to cases in which a soul, wishing to discharge some lingering karmic debt, has volunteered to prepare the way (and the body) for another entity to take over during young adulthood, and perform a specific mission relating to the betterment of mankind.

Before I knew anything about David Hutton's background, the Guides had written: "The present David is a fine person who entered the body as an opportunity to aid his fellow man. In a previous lifetime he had failed in an undertaking to form a community with a large group of like-minded people who would all strive toward the goal of perfection; but funds were unavailable, and in a freak accident he was killed. This time he wanted to get on with that work as quickly as possible, since the times were right for community living and cooperation on a grand scale, due to the approaching shift of the earth on its axis. He therefore gladly entered that body [during the coma, or trancelike sleep], and as time advanced he felt a strong urge that America was the right place to be at the right time, and he subconsciously sensed that the Northwest would provide the most opportunities for the work that he would choose to do. He will in time operate a community center, teaching skills and survival techniques, and will become a much needed leader in the years ahead."

David, with growing assurance of his own awareness, had expressed the belief that my Guides would confirm his assertion that he and his predecessor had made a prenatal agreement to exchange places. I put this question to the Guides, and they wrote: "The original David Hutton is here and asks that his successor remember a time when they met between lives and agreed to the experiment. The present David had been abruptly killed in the accident previously referred to, and was distressed that his life had been cut short in young manhood. The other David was irked that in a previous incarnation he had stayed so long in physical body that he was decrepit and of little use, and was vastly relieved when he was eventually released from that body. In the spirit plane there is no age differential, of course, but the two of them made an agreement of sorts: the former old man to assume the youthful years, and the other the mature and aging ones. Each is a fine person, and David in this go-round will achieve the top leadership role that is rightfully his. Good preparation and good planning all around!"

During a quick trip to Washington, D.C., in late April David called on us, and while reading this chapter he uttered a sharp ejaculation. Intrigued, I asked what had prompted his exclamation, and he responded, "This paragraph about the predecessor in my body having lived too long in a previous lifetime. It explains so much! Before the transferral of egos I remember how fearful I was at the thought of growing old. It was so repulsive to me that I couldn't bear to be around old people. I didn't even want to think about aging, although I was only a youngster. Nowadays I look forward to the future with great zest. I have every intention of surviving the Shift and living to a great age, in service to mankind."

Rather hesitantly, he then commented on the Guides' assertion that in one of his previous lifetimes he had tried to found a Community, but that his life was cut short by a freak accident. "It may sound far-out, but I know my identity in that lifetime," he began. "I was an Essene called Joshua in ancient Israel, and I died at the age of 33. That is probably the explanation for the fact that it took me so long to notice any change after I became a Walk-in this time around. I was 33 years old, two years ago, when I suddenly knew my purpose and changed the entire direction of my life."

David then surprised me by declaring that only

two weeks ago he and a friend had begun arrangements to found a New Age Survival Community in the northwest Panhandle region of Idaho. The Guides say that the area will be a safe one during and after the shift of the earth on its axis, and that in *this* incarnation he will succeed in his Community endeavor.

David says that his wife and his parents are unhappy with his alteration from an ambitious and successful young business executive to one whose chief interest lies in philosophical pursuits to aid the earth and all mankind, but he feels that he is performing his mission.

"I have spent a great deal of time studying to improve my knowledge and awareness in all spiritual areas," he says, "my attention being directed towards the works of Gurdjieff, Ouspensky, the Existentialist philosophers, and Greek, Tibetan and Indian mystics. Whatever I read in this line does not surprise me. I feel that I already know what is written, and that the information is there as an affirmation only. I guess it's the difference between knowingness and knowledge."

As is the case with so many other Walk-ins, David has now separated from his wife, and has moved to Seattle until he can establish his Survival Community.

CHAPTER XVI
COUNT CARNETTE

Long before I had heard of Walk-ins, I began receiving letters in 1977 from a young man named Count Carnette, in Seattle, who identified himself as a concert pianist and a "fan" of my books in the psychic field. Later that year he sent me a first album of his recordings called *Count Carnette Plays. Psychic Piano Music from the Masters.*

The descriptive matter on the back of the album stated that the young black musician has never formally studied the piano since he began playing at the age of three, but feels that the compositions were given to him by Franz Liszt and other masters.

I was, of course, familiar with the well-publicized

case of Rosemary Brown, an English woman who, in 1964, began receiving music that she believed came to her psychically from old masters, and who wrote about it in her book, *Unfinished Symphonies.*

With heightened interest I played the Carnette record on my phonograph, and sensed that the music was indeed inspired. I therefore asked my Guides about this twenty-four-year-old man who, for lack of a musical education, cannot even notate the music that pours through his piano, and they wrote in part: "The man called Count is a sensitive, who will find his greatest source of satisfaction in listening within, where he attunes to the finest sources of melodic harmony. In his last four or five incarnations he was a white man, and is therefore somewhat at a loss to find himself hampered this time around by the society in which he finds himself. You knew him in one of his lives at the French court, where he was a musician of considerable repute. Facile and quick-tongued, he made many friends and a few jealous enemies, and he will see these recurring in this life-time, both friend and foe, for he is still trying to find himself among the society in which he once moved. A splendid talent and a good mind."

I sent a copy of the message to Count, and he responded enthusiastically, but because of my voluminous mail from readers I could not maintain a correspondence with him. The years passed, and although I had not forgotten Count Carnette I could not recall in which city he lived. Then came the memorable stopover in Seattle last February, and because he had read that I would be addressing The Sixth Sense Seminar, we finally met. He had brought me a new album of his music called *The Art of Count Carnette,* and the back cover related that at the age of three he began to play on a toy piano with a color chart positioned above the keyboard. "Each note within the octave corresponded to a color on the chart," he wrote, "so that music was not only audible to me, but visual as well. I found that certain patterns of color produced harmonious sounds, and I distinctly remember the color for each note. In fact, this is how I still find my way upon the keyboard, although it has been many years since I've seen that toy piano."

Continuing, Carnette related that since his family could not afford piano lessons or an instrument, he used to practice on old pianos at hospitals and rest homes, but that while practicing a popular tune in 1974 his hands suddenly began to play a completely unrelated piece of music. "I felt as if my hands were being guided over the keys," he recalled, "and there was another immediate sensation: that of a warm and loving presence in the room. It was the presence of Frédéric Chopin. After telling me who he was, he explained that he and other composers in spirit would come to give me music to share with the world as proof of life beyond what we call death. Chopin's prediction has proven correct, for I have received music from composers such as Liszt, Robert Schumann and Sergei Rachmaninoff, including many others who were not recognized as famous composers during their lifetime."

I was delighted to meet my former pen pal, whom I liked immediately, and on my return home I played his new recording. Unfortunately I have an untrained musical ear, but to me only one word seemed to fit his music . . . *sublime!* At the next morning's session I asked the Guides for further comment on this remarkable young black musician, and they conveyed this exciting message: "Count Carnette is a Walk-in, who as a young boy felt so repelled by his surroundings that he wished to leave, and thus made himself available for a highly skilled pianist who entered that body and replaced the fine young lad who had also been a pianist in previous lifetimes, but could not face the conditions under which he had volunteered to live in this incarnation. He therefore gladly withdrew in favor of a more highly evolved soul, who entered that body to demonstrate what goodness and faith and love of people as well as music could perform, as an example to others."

This, then, was another example of a transferral of egos that occurred in childhood! I wrote to Count in praise of his album, and relayed the new message from the Guides. In his reply, he declared, "It is so seldom that anyone gets to hear the music as *I* hear it. When the masters give it to me it sounds so rich, so full—almost orchestral in nature. But I must play it upon a man-made instrument, and so much is lost." And of the Guides' comments he wrote, "I cannot describe what I felt as I read your Guides' words about my being a Walk-in. I wasn't shocked, just mildly surprised, for it explains so much to me."

Carnette said that he has recently been developing direct-voice channeling from a discarnate who calls himself Dr. Callaeo, and that with his business manager asking the questions, Dr. Callaeo had declared, the evening before: "I wish to tell you that Count Carnette is indeed a Walk-in. He could not cope well with his childhood. It was so unhappy that he wished to be rid of it. There was a spirit of a fine musician who wanted to inhabit the physical body so that he could continue making music, not only for its own sake, but to make music in a way that would harmonize the entire earth plane. He wanted to do a universal work, so there was an agreement between the two souls that they would exchange places. I believe Count could verify that he was extremely fearful as a child. He was less than ten years old when he made the transition, which was effected within a few days. It was one of the rare cases of a Walk-in entering the body of a child, but it was necessary, because the boy was on the verge of a nervous breakdown or suicide."

The manager asked about the goals of the Walk-in, and the reply came: "Part of that goal had to do with healing, not only of the physical body but of the mind and emotions. He had been a musician of great stature on several occasions, particularly in the French court of Louis XIV, and returned with humanitarian goals. Thoughts are so powerful that the present entity has only to desire to heal a particular individual, or a crowd in an auditorium where he plays and sings, and if those people are ready to accept their healing they will be healed."

I suggested to Count Carnette that if he believed himself to be a Walk-in, and was willing to have me report on his case, he should tell me about his childhood and the change that occurred with the transferral of souls.

"Let me tell you why my being a Walk-in can explain so many things," he replied. "I cannot relate to my early childhood much at all. It is as if I were indeed some other person. You asked if I felt then that I would like to withdraw because of unhappiness. I'm positive that I did. You see, I had a very unhappy childhood. There was a lot of suffering, both physical and emotional, involved. I was a battered child. Of course this was done in the name of 'love', but when I had my little wrists tied together, then tied to the post of the bed in preparation for beatings that might last thirty minutes or more, I knew I was being tortured. I actually thought of a torture chamber. What did I know of torture chambers at that young age? A recollection of a past life?

"I know now that my mother had serious emotional problems, and that I had a strange love/hate relationship with her. I had toys and was well clothed, but was kept apart from most of the children in our ghetto neighborhood because they were considered too rough. I was protected, and I clung to my mother because she was the only one who represented security to me. I never knew my father well, as he was a seaman and didn't live with us. I saw him only on a few occasions, and never felt comfortable with him. In fact, I seldom ever felt comfortable except when I was left alone. My mother was very religious. I went to Sunday school and church every Sunday, and afterward had to report on the sermon. If my report did not satisfy Mom, I got a good beating when we reached home. Is it any wonder that I had little interest in Jesus, although there were pictures of Him on every wall in our apartment?"

Carnette told me that he was named Lee William Carnett, Jr., after his father, a white man whose parents were French, and who came to the West Coast from Canada. "I was not my mother's first child," he said. "I have two half brothers and two half sisters, only one of whom I've seen, as they were taken away from my mother by the state and placed in separate foster homes, after neighbors reported their cries and screams of pain."

Count says that he recalls how desperately he wanted to leave his life, but cannot pinpoint the exact time when the exchange of egos occurred. All he knows for sure is that one day he awakened to find himself with less fear, more courage, and a more outgoing nature. As soon as he was old enough to do so he left home, and paid to have his name legally changed to Count Lee William Carnette, adding the *e* on the end of his surname to emphasize his French heritage, which according to the Guides is the dominant influence on the "new" incarnate. I find it interesting to note that long before I knew anything about Carnette's background, when I first queried the Guides about him and his album, they began their discussion by writing: "the man called Count," not "the man named Count."

During my long association with the Guides, they have repeatedly stressed that in the spirit plane there is no such division as race. All of us have been, or will in future incarnations be members of each of the five races, as well as of the major religious sects, and we occasionally change our sex as well, in order to experience every reality before eventually achieving reunion with our Creator.

Count says that he has "never related much" to being black. "When I sing Negro spirituals I am totally black," he muses, "but otherwise I never think of race, and I'm always momentarily startled when someone remarks on my Negro heritage. I know without a doubt that I agreed to don this physical body as a symbol of the white and black—the yin and yang. Just as my work is concerned with universal love, so I needed a body that would serve as a subtle reminder of it."

In speaking of his childhood after the transferral of egos, Carnette recalled that around the age of ten he developed an obsession to own a piano of his own, although it was an impossible dream, as he and his mother were on welfare, and she had "scrimped and saved to send me to a religious school," rather than to the public school in their ghetto. He was excused from physical education classes because of his nervous stomach and asthma, a result of his childhood fears, and while the others were exercising he would stay in the empty classroom to practice on the piano. At school entertainments he would always volunteer to play the piano with other students who were taking piano lessons, but was never invited to do so.

At the age of twelve or thirteen, while visiting a rest home with his mother, he discovered a piano that was hardly ever used, and received permission to practice on it. To his astonishment, the old people would smile and drag up chairs to hear more of his music. "I'm sure I knew instinctively then that this was to be my life work," he said. "I never thought in terms of being famous. I just wanted to make people feel good, and that is still my ambition today."

Count continued to play for residents of rest homes and hospitals throughout grammar and junior high school. He was also allowed to practice thirty minutes a day on a better piano at the Seattle Public Library, and when a woman named Yolanda Mattocks heard of his plight she solicited funds to buy him a secondhand spinet that was presented to the teenager at a talent show in 1966 called Battle of the Bands. He won an award to take a course in music history and literature at the Cornish School of Allied Arts, and after high school graduation in 1970, while working at odd jobs, he gave free concerts and played without fee at numerous civic functions, also continuing to entertain for the elderly at rest homes. Unfortunately he has yet to make a decent living from his music.

In 1974 he had the experience that has changed his life: the presence of Chopin in the room where his hands had unexpectedly begun playing a piece of music that was totally unrelated to his practice work. Subsequently other masters seemed to make their presence felt, and to give him music that they had failed to write while in physical body.

Carnette says of this phenomenon: "I have a tender regard for Liszt. I feel a special rapport with him and recognize him as a loving soul with great patience and understanding. His method of working (with me) is typical. I am given a short section of the piece, which I must memorize [because he does not know how to write it down]. During each sitting I am again given more to memorize. Later I am told exactly where each segment fits into the work as a whole. It was in this manner that the rhapsody [in his second album] was channeled. Robert Schumann's method differs somewhat from that of the other composers. When 'To a Rose' was channeled, we worked nonstop from two A.M. until five A.M. At the end of three hours the entire piece was completely learned and memorized. Later he explained the music to me in detail, and said that it was dedicated to his wife, Clara. He said that in this piece it was his wish to show the many aspects of love: the joy, the sadness, and the intensity."

And where does Count Carnette receive this masterful music, which is giving delight to so many? In the sanctuary of the First Christian Church on Broadway, in Seattle, when, late in the evening after his chores are finished, he can seat himself at the piano near the altar, and let the muses come. Because this talented young artist receives almost no money from his performances as a pianist and vocalist, he works as the security caretaker at the church in exchange for his free rooms there. And the opportunity to play with good acoustics on a fine piano!

Surely a breakthrough is at hand for this brilliant Walk-in about whom William Bryan, professor of music history and piano at Foothill College in California has written: "When one understands the difficulty of playing the piano it is all the more remarkable to realize that as we listen to Count Carnette's muse-inspired pianism we are listening to a self-taught pianist! Have Liszt and Chopin not only spelled out the notes to Mr. Carnette, but instructed him in performance practices as well? It would seem so. Here indeed is a sensitive artist's rendering of music that has come to him from the spheres. Some composers are audacious enough to say the Divine sent them their music. Count Carnette is content to hear from Liszt and the like, to the delight of lovers of piano music."

I asked the Guides for any final word about Count Carnette, and they wrote: "He came into the body he now occupies before the age of puberty, when the other entity became so discouraged with life that he simply withdrew. A period of long sleep after a severe knocking about, and the present soul entered. This soul was a court pianist and composer in the court of Louis XIV, a virtuoso who had also been a musician in previous lifetimes. He has returned again and again as a musician, and has known Liszt, Rachmaninoff and Schumann in past incarnations. He will go far!" And how I hope that the recognition so long delayed will soon be coming for him.

CHAPTER XVII
RUTH SODERSTROM

By now I thought that I had encountered every type
of transition by which a Walk-in could enter a body
that was being vacated by another. I had conducted
lengthy interviews with some who had entered at
clinical death or during near-death experiences, and
with others who had effected the transferral while
floating out-of-the-body, or during coma or sleep.

Then I had the good fortune to talk with a wise
and wonderful Walk-in who had apparently entered
the body of a weak and vacillating woman while the
latter was wide awake, but desperate to leave.

Although I did not meet Ruth Soderstrom that
eventful day in Seattle when I discovered so many

other Walk-ins, I later learned that she was there, and had brought thirty-five students from her Psychic Energy Center in Tacoma to attend my lecture. Afterward I began hearing about a remarkably sage counselor-instructor in Tacoma who exhibited every sign of being a Walk-in, and upon asking the Guides about her was told that she is a particularly fine example of one who made an unusual transition, because of a pressing need for her services.

It was Shirlee Teabo, that joyously open-hearted, kindly, vivacious redhead, to whom I turned for help in locating Ruth Soderstrom, and as usual Shirlee established the contact. Then our interviews began, but I was somewhat startled when Ruth declared that if she is indeed a Walk-in, the transition occurred within seconds, during a long-distance telephone call six years ago. Could such a soul transferral actually happen with such suddenness, while the Walk-out was awake and aware?

The Guides' answer to that question was a resounding yes. Writing of Mrs. Soderstrom, who is now sixty-three years old, they declared: "She is a particularly fine person who is doing much to guide others in their crossovers, even as she adjusts to her own transferral of egos. She is correct that it happened all at once, but the new entity had been around the former occupant for some time, because the one who withdrew was so depressed that she despaired of her life. Many, many times she had yearned to leave her physical body and return to the spirit state."

Without relaying this message from the Guides, I asked Ruth Soderstrom if she had ever wanted to die before that strange telephone call, and she replied, "Oh, Ruth, so many, many times! I can't tell you how often I had wanted to go." She then recounted for me the story of that unhappy life, and of its apparent futility and purposelessness, before the transferral of egos that has since established her as one of the most admired women in that area of the Northwest.

Ruth Tapp was born in Port Orchard, Washington, to a navy yard welder and his wife, but shortly thereafter the family "pulled up stakes and moved to a Christian community" that was dedicated to religious living. Ruth's education ended with the ninth grade, and during the succeeding decades she married four times, giving birth to three girls and three boys during the first three of those marriages.

"My idea of a good time was to go dancing and 'get high' every Saturday night with my husband and friends," she recalls ruefully. "I was tired of responsibilities, and when my middle daughter Vernell's teenage marriage broke up, I told her she'd made her own bed and could now lie in it."

As time passed Mrs. Soderstrom was aware that Vernell had become addicted to alcohol and drugs, and in 1970 she was committed to a mental institution after having tried to commit suicide by slitting her wrists with a razor blade. What she did not know was that Vernell had subsequently escaped from the institution and disappeared. "I was so frustrated in my fourth marriage, and so buried in my own concerns that I simply lost contact with her. I told myself I had all I could handle with my own problems. I remember a number of times wishing that I could die and start all over again, because I felt so trapped and useless."

She had not heard from Vernell for six years, when one day in January 1976 the telephone rang. It was her daughter, crying hysterically. Unable at first to talk, she finally blurted out, "Oh, Mom, Mom, I'm a hopeless alcoholic. I've tried so hard to quit drinking and I can't. If you're ever going to be a mother to me, please help me now."

Reliving that tragic scene, Mrs. Soderstrom said to me, "Ruth, there is no way I can express what happened then. My husband was standing a few feet away and, realizing what the conversation was all about, he announced that if I let Vernell come to our house, he would leave me. The thought of the insecurity, of being on my own and facing all these problems alone, was more than I could stand. My whole life passed before my eyes, and I sure wasn't proud of it. I'd been so weak, always taking the easy way out of every situation that I got myself into! I took a long despairing breath, and suddenly I heard words coming out of my mouth that I didn't think I was speaking: 'Vernell, you come on home, honey, and I'll do all I can to help you.' Suddenly I felt a calm strength starting in my solar plexus and flooding throughout my body. I have never had such a powerful feeling before or since, and I have not been the same person since that moment. I now react to challenges in a positive, affirmative way, and my love and concern for others has increased one hundred percent. Before, it was nil."

Vernell had an old car that she wanted to keep, so she started driving to the home of her mother and stepfather in Tacoma. Two days later a stranger telephoned Mrs. Soderstrom to say that she had discovered Vernell crying helplessly on the freeway, beside her broken-down car. The woman had taken her to a motel ninety miles south of Tacoma, and when Ruth arrived she found her daughter passed out on the bed, with an empty wine bottle hidden under the mattress.

"As Vernell began to sober up, her body started twisting with what I later learned was drug-withdrawal cramps," Ruth continued. "She had planned to get off the drugs with my help, and had brought along only enough for the trip. Then, with all the delays caused by car trouble, she had run out of them, so she'd bought the bottle of wine to relieve the cramps. I undressed her and got her into a tub of warm water, but was horrified to see her chest and back scars from self-administered wounds. She had been such a beautiful girl, and now she looked twice her age of thirty-five. The next night I got her home and settled into the guest room, but I couldn't sleep. I kept seeing her scarred and twisted body. Suddenly I had a vision of a huge catlike animal breaking out of a cocoon in the shadows, and heard a voice say, 'Don't be alarmed. Only the cocoon is damaged. The butterfly will emerge unscathed.' It was like a dream, yet I was awake; and I can't express the comfort that the vision gave me in the years ahead, when Vernell would alternate between periods of alcoholism and drugs, followed by stomach-pumping, and then weeks of being free of them. She would try so hard to lick the addiction, but then she would meet another man and go off with him for months at a time. She couldn't seem to live without the man-woman relationship, and that would set her off on drugs and liquor again. Through it all, I couldn't believe the strength and energy that I had. Nurses would prick her body with a pin, and there was no response. Once I sat up all night in the hospital beside her comatose body, and then went directly to the University of Puget Sound and gave a slide lecture on my experiences while training with psychic surgeons in the Philippine Islands.

"When Vernell would come back to the house, I would work with her, and a deep love developed between us. At first I gave her numerology readings, but after I discovered regressive hypnosis I would take her through a relaxing method back to past life experiences, trying to determine the cause of her present addiction. In one life she had been a healer, but in many, many others she committed suicide because she couldn't handle her impulsive responses to crises."

I have heard a number of these hypnotic sessions that were recorded on tape, and in one of them she was screaming in anguish because a boy had killed her baby, while she was pregnant with another child. In some she seemed to be contacting a wise old sage, and she was dispensing wisdom, and also describing the creation of the earth and mankind.

Three months after the telephone call that dramatically changed Ruth's life, Vernell had just described a past-life death under hypnosis, when she announced: "I see some caves. I'm a student, and I came to learn forgiveness. I'm coming into the body of a ten-year-old boy. He's dying. I want to be him, so that I can learn to forgive. I don't want to wait to be born." Then, after a short silence, she added, "The soul is me now."

Mrs. Soderstrom says of that moment when the words were first spoken, "Ruth, I was horrified and shocked. I was repelled at the idea. I swept it under the rug, and didn't even discuss it with Vernell after she came out of her altered state of consciousness. Then, when *Strangers Among Us* came out three years later, and I heard people discussing the concept of Walk-ins, I couldn't wait to read it. I found the theory very fascinating, and I could not help but notice how my own experience fit the criteria you had laid out for a Walk-in. And after my daughter's discussion under hypnosis of entering another's body, which I knew she couldn't have fabricated, I realized that such a thing as Walk-ins was entirely possible."

Ruth said her own theory had been that "everyone is composed of many aspects of consciousness, some higher and some lesser evolved, but all are fragments of the huge gestalt of universal consciousness that we call God, and to which we are striving to return; and since we are all part of one consciousness, who's to say where mine ends and yours begins." She has obviously given the matter much thought, and has decided that the difference between the two concepts is only one of terminology.

Mrs. Soderstrom's hypnotic sessions with her daughter, as well as her study with some psychic surgeons in the Philippines, received local publicity and she was invited to speak at churches, high schools, and area colleges. Then in 1979 she was asked to teach a class at the community college, entitled "Discovering Your Psychic Energies," and the course proved so popular that it developed into several classes. The attendance became so great that a Tacoma paper wrote a favorable review of her teachings, which were concerned with spiritual growth and evolvement, but some of the civic leaders irately condemned it as witchcraft, and the city-owned college was forced to discontinue the courses. Then the students began coming to her house, begging Ruth to continue teaching them there.

"My husband's attitude fluctuated between pride and resentment at the overwhelming response to my work," she mused. "The crowds were too large for our small house, and he suggested that we buy a larger one that would accommodate classrooms. The students were jubilant, and with their help I found a big old house that would be perfect for the endeavor. I kept my fingers crossed, even while the students were naming the venture Psychic Energy Center, because I knew my husband's changeable moods; but the students had even painted a large sign with the new name on it when my husband announced, 'There's no way that I will ever buy a house for other people.' Before I realized that the words were out, I replied, 'In no way can I spend my life living the self-centered one that you choose to live.' Ruth, I'd been wanting to say that for years, and now the words asking for a divorce were out. My eighteen-year marriage was at an end, and it was frightening to think of being on my own, with so little money for mortgage payments and food."

Mrs. Soderstrom said that she prayed and meditated about her decision, and as she did so she saw an eye in the distance, which grew larger as it approached her. Then it was displaced by a picture of Jesus, and while she was trying to "hang on" to the vision of Christ, she saw it suddenly replaced by a robed man with very dark hair and a beard. She could not recognize him, but he looked at her with loving compassion, and then vanished.

Ruth had sensed that she was receiving outside direction ever since the telephone call from her daughter, because she had sought none of the strange occurrences that led to the founding of the center. Then one day a book called *Secrets from Mount Shasta* fell into her hands, and upon opening it she saw a picture of the dark, bearded man who had come to her in the vision. "Ruth, it was as if a shot of electricity went through my body," she recalls. The book by Earlyne Chaney identified the man in the picture as Kut-hu-mi, the Ascended Master who inspired Astara, an organization based on ancient Egyptian mystery teachings. He was also a founding master of the Theosophical Society, and he is said to work for "healing and peace throughout the world."

Vernell died recently of alcoholism, but her mother feels that through the wisdom spoken during her hypnotic regressions the young woman gained tremendous spiritual growth, and became an instrument in helping others. "Only the cocoon was damaged," Ruth says, in referring to her earlier vision. "I see her now as a beautiful butterfly, freed from her terrible addiction. We are all on the road back to cosmic consciousness. We must all practice understanding, tolerance, and unconditional love.

That's what life has taught me, and what I'm trying to teach others."

I asked the Guides for any further information about this remarkable woman who underwent such complete metamorphosis during a telephone conversation, and they wrote: "In a previous lifetime she was a seer in Persia, and in another a sage in ancient Egypt. She has long prepared for this advent to assist with the preparations for the shift of the earth on its axis, as she was instrumental in saving many lives at the time of the Atlantean deluge. Her voice will indeed be heard in the years ahead."

CHAPTER XVIII

THRESHOLD TO TOMORROW

Planet Earth is currently on the cusp between the Piscean and Aquarian Ages, and just as a person born on the cusp between two astrological signs is said to reflect some characteristics of both, so we earthlings are precariously balanced between the materialism of recent centuries and the idealism of the future.

We are indeed on the threshold of a New Age, which the Guides say will be ushered in by a shift of the earth on its axis at the close of this century. Our globe is spinning its way out of the water sign denoted by a fish, the symbol by which early Christians identified themselves to each other, and into the air sign of Aquarius, when we will be able to communicate as easily by thought as by the spoken word.

The Guides foresee one more brutalizing war in this century, unless herculean efforts are exerted by people of goodwill to avert it. Then comes the New Age, fulfilling the biblical prophecy of a thousand years of peace and the second coming of the Christ Spirit to establish God's kingdom on earth.

It is to prepare us for these awesome events that Walk-ins are said to be returning at a rate unprecedented since the dawn of recorded history. They wish to alert us to potential dangers, and teach us how to prepare ourselves not only for survival in physical body, but for our eventual crossover into the spirit plane. They are our friends, and because of the greater awareness that they bring directly from spirit, they are more farsighted than most of us. Their mission is humanitarian, and they are so highly energized that almost any problem to them seems surmountable.

One of their goals is to forestall World War III, and if enough like-minded people around the world will meditate and work for peace, it can be prevented. The Guides are highly in favor of the psychic seminars that are mushrooming throughout the world, and say of them: "They are good for bringing to a focus the love of all humanity with the Creative Force of the universe. If people meditate together they are releasing energies that help to move the mountains of fear and anger." All of us have free will, except where it conflicts with universal law. In other words, the Guides say that we cannot prevent the shift of the earth on its axis, which is inevitable and will provide a cleansing process for Mother Earth. War is *not* inevitable, but unless we exert our free will to prevent it, they have predicted that World War III will begin around 1986 in the area of Ethiopia and spread rapidly, engulfing the planet in the white heat of blazing bullets.

In preparing this final chapter, I hopefully asked the Guides if they now foresee a brighter picture for the remainder of this century than their predictions in *Strangers Among Us*. They replied: "The war will begin as foreseen, unless there is a tremendous rallying of the public will. Leaders often see advantages in such actions, to divert attention from domestic problems, and it is only the burdened people and those of goodwill who can prevent such a debacle. Mengistu [head of state Mengistu Haile Mariam] still looks like the man, and Ethiopia the place for the initial fray that will rapidly swell into a world confrontation. The time is ripe to begin planning survival communities that will enjoy tremendous popularity in the decades ahead, as people sicken of city life with its sterility of spiritual purpose and flee to the rural areas, where they can join like-minded people in raising their own crops, canning and drying foods, and finding intellectual stimulation in meditating and working together. These cooperative ventures will be of enormous benefit when patches of famine arise, and if war comes will produce quantities of food that otherwise would not be available. They are superb training grounds for New Age people who will work harmoniously and strive to raise the potential of the human spirit in each of those who participates. As for the fighting, if it occurs it will not go beyond the early 1990s, as said before, and will not involve the big nuclear weapons so rightly feared.

"Signs of the coming shift will begin to appear later in that decade, as scientists probe with new instruments and discover signs of increased wobbling on the earth's orbit around the sun. There are those who will discount the public anxiety, but others will begin to prepare for the removal of the population to safe areas inland, away from high tension wires and towering structures."

In this connection, it is interesting to note an Associated Press item of June 11, 1981, which quotes Dr. Gernot Winkler, head of the time division at the U.S. Naval Observatory as saying that the earth's rotation has recently speeded up, and that this fact "at least temporarily reverses the long-term slowing trend of the earth."

A number of my readers have written to remind me that in *Strangers Among Us,* written four years ago, the Guides warned: "The weather will become increasingly violent, with heavy snowfalls, strong gales, and increased humidity." Certainly the winter of 1981–1982 fulfilled that prophecy, with the record-breaking cold in North America and Europe that destroyed much of the citrus, peach, and apple crops, and the unprecedented snows and gale winds. They say of the times ahead: "Snowfalls will increase as more moisture becomes trapped in the earth's inner atmosphere and winds come howling down out of the arctic. Summer will shorten for those in the Northern Hemisphere, and as the time nears for the shift, there will be noticeable changes in atmospheric pressure. Several years before the actual shift, scientists will be taking soundings and speaking of an increased wobbling of the earth. Volcanoes will erupt in several areas of the North American continent, as well as in the Caribbean and Mediterranean areas, and earthquakes will register more frequently on the Richter scale."

Intrigued by the Guides' earlier assertion that a Walk-in will become president of the United States later in this century, I asked what particular role he would play, and they replied: "The Walk-in president will be able to put into effect safety measures for the citizens of the United States in preparation for the shift. He will designate sections to which the population can go at the first signs of earth wobble, and prepare supplies of food and shelter. There will be growing recognition that the shift is in prospect, and through his inner awareness the president will sense the areas to which those who want to survive in physical body should be directed.

"The weather alterations at the present time are due to wind patterns that are already beginning to shift, and also to the pollutants in the atmosphere that ward off the sun's warming rays and collect moisture that is unable to rise to sufficient heights, as formerly. The ozone layer is adversely affected by the pollutants and sprays, and as the end of the century approaches this condition will adversely affect earthlings in large numbers."

I urged the Guides to begin now to enumerate some of the safe areas, so that readers can make long-term plans if they so wish, and they replied:

"Safe areas will generally be away from the coastal regions with barriers of mountains between the secure land and the seas that will experience tremendous tidal waves. Some sections will sink of their own accord, so not all protected areas can be termed safe. Since some volcanoes will erupt in Mexico, Central America, and elsewhere, it is difficult at this time to foresee just where the destruction of the land as we know it will occur. Canada, except in coastal areas, will be largely secure, as will much of the central portion of America and the Great Northwest behind the Coastal Mountains. Europe will have its problems, because so much of the coastline is indented with small harbors and low-lying lands. The Scandinavian peninsula will enlarge, although at the time of the shift inhabitants should stay away from the coast because of high winds and tides. England will disappear, as will Holland and other nearby coastal regions. The northern parts of Russia and China will be secure, as we have said, and in the Southern Hemisphere some of the land areas will rapidly expand in dimension."

I asked particularly about New Zealand and Australia, because so many from there write to ask me about their homelands, and the Guides said that both will increase in size as land rises from the sea. They said this will also be true of Fiji, but some of the Pacific islands, including Hawaii, will disappear with the shifting of the present sea bottom. "Canada and Russia will become warmer, as will parts of the United States, but other parts of it will become colder, as the earth skews about on the axis. South America will experience earth tremors and drastic alterations in formation as the Andes flatten at some points and shock tremors reduce certain land masses. The South Pole will be in a part of South America after the shift, and as Lemuria partly emerges again from the Pacific Ocean, some of it will be frigid and some salubrious. Antarctica will become a new and larger land mass in a more temperate climate, and that is about all that we foresee at this time."

Well, wait a minute! How could both Canada and Russia become warmer? Surely in an earth shift that brought more temperate climate to one of them, the other would encompass the new North Pole. At this point I brought out my globe of the earth and began playing with it. Aha! If our planet indeed "skews about" or "slurps to the side," as the Guides have previously said, then this could most certainly occur.

At our next daily session I questioned the Guides about it, and they replied: "The South Pole will be in the southern part of South America, and the North Pole in the Pacific Ocean at some point that we are unable now to pinpoint. As to Russia and Canada both becoming warmer, if you roll the globe in your hands you will see that this is feasible. As to the United States becoming warmer in some sections and colder in others, the east and west of the country will be in different latitudes. Indiana will be in one of the safer areas, as will Oklahoma, Arkansas, and Illinois, except where the latter approaches the Mississippi, as that corridor leading down from the Great Lakes will become a river bed."

Readers of my previous books in the psychic field are aware that the Guides have been remarkably accurate in their predictions, but in *Strangers Among Us* they made two errors. They correctly foresaw that Jimmy Carter would win the nomination and election, and would serve only one term, and that the Shah of Iran would be deposed. But they erred in saying that a "big-spending Democrat" would succeed Carter, and that the Shah would spend his declining years in Europe.

When I asked them about this, they wrote: "As to Ronald Reagan as successor to Carter, it was there all the time for us to see, but we inadvertently looked too far ahead, as we were viewing the next two decades. We foresaw the 'results' of a big-spending Democrat who will nearly bankrupt the American economy, but it was to occur after Reagan's one term in the White House. Voters exercised their free will in the closing days of the 1980 election to choose a man who would try to stem the tide of free-spending government, but unless they again do so, we see the Democrat of whom we earlier spoke reversing the Reagan trend. As to the Shah of Iran, he was not foreordained to pass over when he did, but he lost his will to live. Cancer and other debilitating diseases are as much in mental attitude as in physical body, and he had lost the will to live, feeling betrayed by the United States and other powers. Broken in spirit, he willed himself to return to the spirit plane."

As related in previous books, I meet the Guides each morning at nine o'clock, and after a brief period of meditation rest my fingers lightly on the typewriter keys. Then, with my eyes still closed, the writing begins. I often caution those who would like to attempt automatic writing to do so only at the same hour each day, which establishes a date with a high-minded Guide or Group. I have also recommended that they murmur a brief prayer for protection, because once we have raised our vibrations sufficiently to contact the spirit plane while in the alpha state, it is as easy for an evil entity to reach us as it is for a benign one.

My own prayer is this: "Dear Lord, please protect me from evil and evil entities, and let only good and truth come through." Having been a newspaper writer for thirty-five years, I have a deep dread of misleading the public, and on the morning of April 5, 1982, I must have murmured the latter part of that prayer with more than usual fervor, because the writing began as follows:

"Ruth, we try at all times to tell you nothing but the truth, the absolute truth, but we are not totally infallible because we are not yet perfected souls. We are striving to carry out the mission to which we pledged ourselves, to demonstrate the fact that there is no barrier between the living and those in spirit; that in fact we are all one, whether in physical or etheric body, and that the striving for perfection is a natural outcropping of our unquenchable longing to return to the source of our energy, our being—the reunion with our Creator. We all began there once as parts of that great Power, and our love for the Creator is greater than our love of self, since we are each but a fragment of the whole. Therefore we wish never to mislead anyone, since each of us is a part of the whole, and as such we are fragments of each other. When we occasionally make an error, we are simply misinterpreting the outcome or overlooking the exercise of free will, which has been given to man to exercise in beneficial ways. If we see a catastrophe ahead, it is possible for us to miss an intermediate occurrence that contributes to the outcome. From our vantage point we can see much farther ahead than when in the physical dimension, and to that extent the future is laid out before us."

The Guides have previously likened the spirit plane, where they are, to the pilot of an airplane, who from above can see much farther ahead than can those of us in physical body, who are like paddlers of a canoe, whose forward vision is limited to the next bend in the river. And I, too, am sometimes an imperfect receiver of the messages from the Guides.

The Guides say of the Walk-ins: "The need is urgent for highly developed souls to provide leadership in this rudderless world, which at times seems to seesaw between despair and blind hope. These are times when leadership needs to assert itself with new approaches to old problems, and never before has there been greater urgency than now, with the shift approaching in less than two decades, as man measures time. The Walk-ins discussed in this book will become leaders, because they keenly sense the inner requirements for helping others to help themselves."

They say that Walk-ins have returned to help those in the flesh during the turbulent years ahead by instilling courage, compassion, love, and cooperation, and are searching out safe areas and means of transportation for those who wish to remain in physical being. Their purpose is altruistic, and they are also eager to help those who will be passing into spirit by infusing them with love of God and mankind. They will be heard from increasingly as this decade progresses toward the shift of the earth on its axis. Many of them are interested in improving the health of survivors, and Jason Winters is one of these. Some want to ease the trauma and despair of those approaching physical death. Others, such as Elizabeth Nachman and Carol Parrish, want to improve the quality of life and arrange safe havens for those who are now dancing in the sun, instead of readying themselves and their families for the alterations to come. Dick Sutphen, David Paladin, and Robert Ranjel are eager to help mankind achieve its potential by understanding the interaction between the spirit and physical planes, and those like Björn Örtenheim want to help people utilize the unused portions of their mind and spirit. If war occurs there will be famine, destitution and bloodshed, and because the Walk-ins were alerted to that probability while still in spirit, they are actively seeking peaceful solutions. It is important that the general population be made aware of their helpful activities, so that leadership is provided and preparations made.

The Guides point out that although some survival communities are already prepared to provide food and shelter for a mass exodus from the cities, others are thinking only in terms of their own preservation and soul advancement. "This, then, is the problem," they say. "They should be thinking not so much of saving self as of helping to ease the hardship of others, for when we understand what soul advancement is all about we realize that the best way to advance is to love others and help them along the way. These cooperative communities, just as Elizabeth is trying to do, should be thinking in terms of mass feedings and shelter, and there is little time to be wasted in preparing for these events. They should look to their larders and their potentials, but beware of those that are stocking guns! That is not the way to help others, but rather the way to look out for Number One.

"We hope that what we are saying will inspire the realization of a national conscience as well as a group conscience. There is light on the horizon, and if war is to be avoided there will have to be a cadre of political thinkers and doers who avert these crises and smooth the troubled waters between nations. With so many Walk-ins assembling now throughout the earth, there is a possibility that they will find themselves in positions where they are able to put the lid on the simmering cauldrons of war."

The Guides lay such stress on the importance of community living that I asked them one morning to discuss that aspect in more detail. They wrote: "Those who elect to begin now to look about for survival or New Age communities should bear in mind that the way will not be easy. It is not painless to learn to live in cooperation with others, exchanging foods and opportunities and sharing skills, but there is a satisfaction in it that has not been known since the early days before industrialization, when it was common practice for those with varying abilities to pitch in and help each other. In that way a cottage became a reality, or a field was plowed, or food exchanged by barter for other skills belonging to those with no acreage or talent for growing foodstuffs. It was a deeper satisfaction by far than sitting on assembly lines in a complex factory operation, or shuffling papers from one desk to another in skyscraper offices. Mankind began in close cooperation, and as living became more complex individuals had less contact with other contributors to the common good, because work was varied and their paths seldom crossed with those in different trades.

"This, then, is the opportunity for human beings again to learn fellowship along with productivity, and the inner satisfactions outweigh the problems of agreeing one with another. For some it will be a joyous period, and for others an irritant, but those suited for community cooperation will forge ahead, so that when the difficult times are upon you, they will be equipped as leaders to point the way. Some will not choose at this time to alter their current lifestyles, and that also is understandable, but they would do well in their spare time to be learning useful skills that do not require electricity. This is a necessity for survivors when the shift occurs, and power lines are demolished; and the storing of seeds, dried foods, tools, fishing reels and other paraphernalia for the simple life will be invaluable."

Another day the Guides wrote that all of us should be learning or teaching manual skills: "How to build and erect without power tools, how to grow and preserve foods, how to dry or tin them, how to memorize truths and wisdoms that are now in printed form, so that they will not be forgotten. Microfilms of books and documents should be secreted in safe havens, with well-circulated memos on where the material is stored, lest it be lost for many thousands of years, as it was in the sinking of Atlantis. There will be large areas of America remaining, including the Northwest behind the Sierra-Cascade Coastal range, substantial sections of the central and mountain states, New England away from the coast, the South away from the coastal areas. But remember that after the shift the Great Lakes will empty through the Mississippi basin to the Gulf, so some of the land in that area will be inundated as the shift alters the slope of the continent."

The Guides said that our changing weather patterns are already signaling the approach of the shift. "Spring will almost vanish," they declared, "as winter plunges into summer, and the summers are foreshortened. At the time of the shift, vast areas will be so altered weatherwise that discontent will be widespread. Thermal underwear will be a commonplace rather than a sports item, and after the shift will become a dire necessity in many areas that were previously temperate or torrid. A good item to stock, along with the seeds and manual tools!"

On an upbeat note, the Guides say that most of the babies being born in the last five years or so are Lemurians, those spiritual, peace-loving inhabitants of the lost continent in the Pacific Ocean who invented the science of agriculture, and whom the Guides described at length in *The World Before*. The warlike, power-hungry, latter-day Atlanteans who have dominated the world's population in the twentieth century are heading into an eclipse, and as more Lemurians return to physical body they will enlighten the New Age. According to my spirit pen pals, most of the current Walk-ins are Lemurians, but not all of them, "for there were good people in

Atlantis too, along with the world troublemakers."
They added that after the initial chaos following the
shift, "the Lemurians, who by then will have popu-
lated so much of the earth, will set to work with glad
hearts to help one another and instill love in the
hearts of those who survive.

"The New Age will bring joy and happiness unex-
celled since the early days of the Atlantean era, when
Lemuria was also still thriving, and when hearts were
pure and ideals lofty. Those who survive the shift
will be a different type of people from those in physical form today, freed from strife and hatred, longing to be of service to the whole of mankind and
eager to serve the Creator. Those souls who helped
to bring on the chaos of the present century will
have passed into spirit to rethink their attitudes, and
the new race will engage in peaceful pursuits and the
uplifting of spirit. Their minds will be open to the
reality of one world, so that they will easily communicate with those in spirit who have not yet found
vehicles [new babies] for earthly entry, but who will
be able to help guide and plan with those who are
cleansing and purifying the earth after the storm
and fury of the shift.

"They will bring in with them the awareness of life
beyond the grave and the realization that it is simply
a matter of vibratory levels, whether one inhabits an
etheric or a physical body. Communication barriers
between the two realms will be erased, for there are
no barriers when one learns to open himself to the
universal law. For those who begin now to prepare
themselves for this time, there will be sure knowledge of how to preserve physical life if they so de-

sire. It will be a wondrous era, and this condition is possible to achieve even in the dying twentieth century. It need not await the shift, for if love is given, cooperation is almost automatic, and wars would be as unthinkable as cannibalism."

The Guides say that they see no reason to change the predictions they made in *Strangers Among Us* about the Antichrist, who is said to be a schoolboy living in a Maryland suburb of Washington, D.C., or of the Second Coming of Christ in the twenty-first century after the Antichrist is overcome. They still foresee the sinking of Manhattan Island and California at the time of the shift, with the latter having previously lost some of its land to the sea.

To wind up this account of the times to come, I asked whether communication in the New Age will be possible between inhabitants of the earth and life forms in outer space, and the Guides declared: "The so-called space aliens are already inspecting your readiness for the shift, as it is obvious from their highly developed instruments that the earth is preparing to wobble and shift on its axis. They are intent on preventing any dislocation of the orbiting patterns of other solar bodies, and wish to dilute the pollutants from planet Earth that are reaching into the stratosphere. When the new race of which we have spoken [the Lemurians] populates the earth in large measure after the shift, there will be stellar intercommunication. Björn Örtenheim is correct in saying that giant sounding instruments are unnecessary for achieving that communication, and they will devise an apparatus that can pick up messages from outer space. Whether there will be visitations between planets in the centuries ahead is not for us to say, but contact will be established."

Prompted by a query from one of my youthful readers, I asked whether beings from outer space worship the same God that we do, and the Guides replied: "As for God, or the Creative Force that fashioned all things through the Word, there is but one God, with many helpers, so that although Jesus, the son, came to Planet Earth, in various Christ forms other embodiments of the Creator have visited other planes and planets. God is all powerful. He is God."

Reverting to our earlier discussion of contact between planetary systems, they continued: "As we have said, there is one Creator of the entire universe with many assistants, and through intermediaries such communication is possible. The extraterrestrials are also souls that began as sparks from the Creator, and as such are not so different from earthlings, although atmospheric conditions and geological variations in their planets have fashioned different physical types. We are all one. That is the message and the truth."

To those few orthodox believers who have written to sound the Old Testament warning against consorting with spirits, I would like to point out that in the New Testament, First Epistle of John 4:1-2, it is written: "*Try* the spirits whether they are of God: because many false prophets are gone out into the world. Hereby know ye the Spirit of God: Every spirit that confesseth that Jesus Christ is come in the flesh is of God."

Certainly my particular Guides, who sign themselves "Lily, Art, and the Group," have from the beginning of our contact a quarter of a century ago firmly identified Jesus Christ as the son of God, who was born to Mary. I had intended to close with that thought, but apparently the Guides decided to have the last word on the subject. It happened to be Easter Sunday, a day made to order for a former Christian minister of the Gospel like Arthur Ford, the renowned medium who joined my circle of Guides after his demise in January 1971. The weather was glorious, after the unseasonable blizzards of previous weeks, and they began their message by writing: "What a beautiful Easter Sunday on this beautiful earth. How it reminds us of that ennobling day when the tomb was found empty, and the miracle of eternal life was proclaimed for the world to see.

"Thank you for the biblical quote about spirits, and remember that we are there with you in spirit as in flesh. Tell those with doubts that Thomas too became a believer when he inserted his fingers in the wounds. Others were able to believe without that physical proof, and for them the glory is greater. We live. We are eternal. We are all wayfarers on our return voyage to the Creator from whence we began. Good sailing!"

Thus ends our current look along the vast corridors of time.

APPENDIX

Readers who wish to contact any of the following people discussed in this book may write to them at the addresses given below. Please remember to enclose a stamped, self-addressed envelope if you are requesting a reply from them or from me.

Count Carnette
1632 Broadway
Seattle, WA 98122

Barbara Easton
1015 S. 30th Court
Renton, WA 98055

Elizabeth Nachman
ASD & R
PO Box 8
Salem, AR 72576

David Paladin
Workshops
Box 11942
Albuquerque, NM 87192

Carol Parrish
Sparrow Hawk Village
PO Box 1274
Tahlequah, OK 74464

Robert Ranjel and Shirlee Teabo
The Sixth Sense
226 S. 312th Street
Federal Way, WA 98003

Ruth Soderstrom
Psychic Energy Center
1912 E. 72nd Street
Tacoma, WA 98404

Jason Winters
Suite 235
4055 Spencer Street
Las Vegas, NV 89101

RECOMMENDED READING

Banerjee, Dr. H. N. *The Once and Future Life.* New York: Dell Publishing Co., 1979.

Colson, Charles W. *Born Again.* Lincoln, Va.: Chosen Books, 1976.

el-Sadat, Anwar. *In Search of Identity.* New York: Harper & Row, 1977.

Self Help Update, Summer/Fall 1981, Scottsdale, Arizona: Valley of the Sun.

Sutphen, Dick. *Past Lives, Future Loves.* New York: Pocket Books, 1978.

————. *You Were Born Again to Be Together.* New York: Pocket Books, 1976.

Weisman, Alan. *We, Immortals.* Phoenix: Valley of the Sun, 1977.

Winters, Jason. *Killing Cancer.* Las Vegas: M and R Publishing Co., 1980.